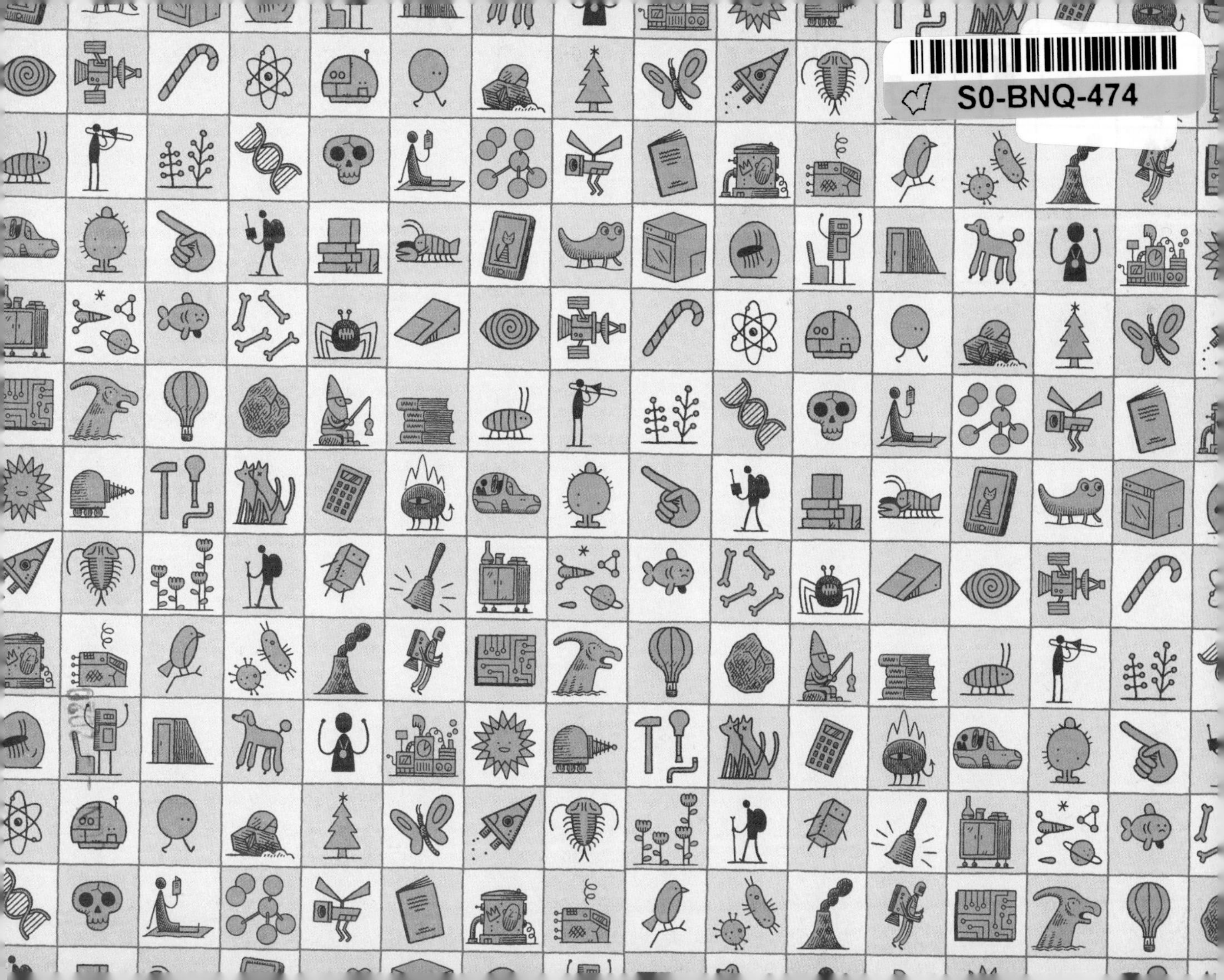

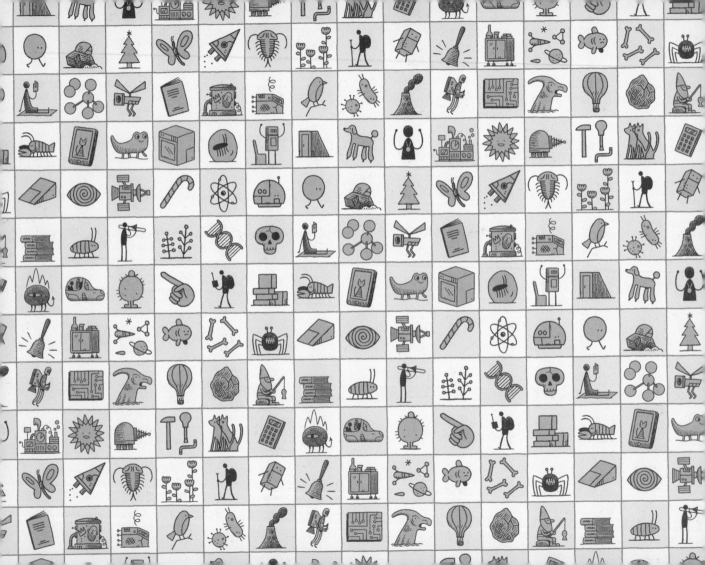

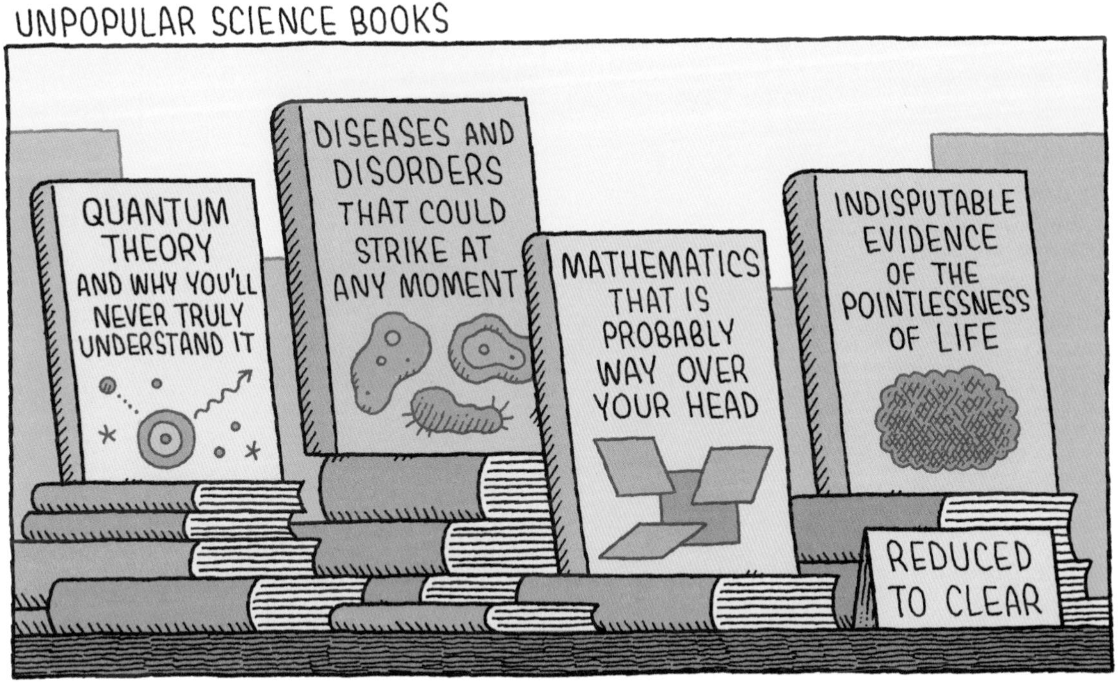
UNPOPULAR SCIENCE BOOKS
QUANTUM THEORY AND WHY YOU'LL NEVER TRULY UNDERSTAND IT
DISEASES AND DISORDERS THAT COULD STRIKE AT ANY MOMENT
MATHEMATICS THAT IS PROBABLY WAY OVER YOUR HEAD
INDISPUTABLE EVIDENCE OF THE POINTLESSNESS OF LIFE
REDUCED TO CLEAR

CARTOONS ORIGINALLY PUBLISHED IN NEW SCIENTIST.

DRAWNANDQUARTERLY.COM

978-1-77046-375-2

FIRST EDITION: APRIL 2020
PRINTED IN CHINA
10 9 8 7 6 5 4 3 2 1

CATALOGUING DATA AVAILABLE FROM
LIBRARY AND ARCHIVES CANADA

PUBLISHED IN THE USA BY DRAWN & QUARTERLY,
A CLIENT PUBLISHER OF FARRAR, STRAUS AND GIROUX

PUBLISHED IN CANADA BY DRAWN & QUARTERLY,
A CLIENT PUBLISHER OF RAINCOAST BOOKS

DEPARTMENT OF MIND-BLOWING THEORIES

CARTOONS BY
TOM GAULD

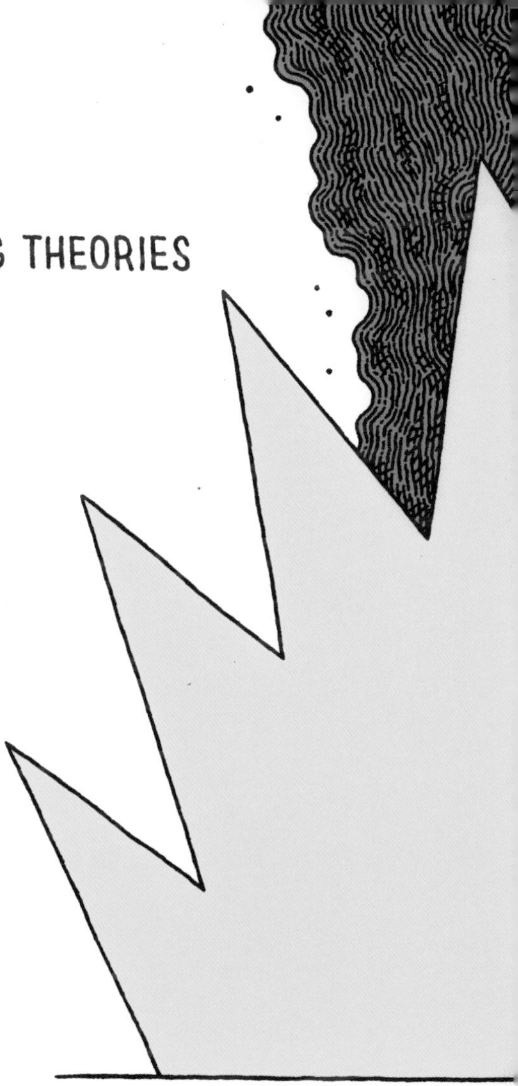

DRAWN & QUARTERLY

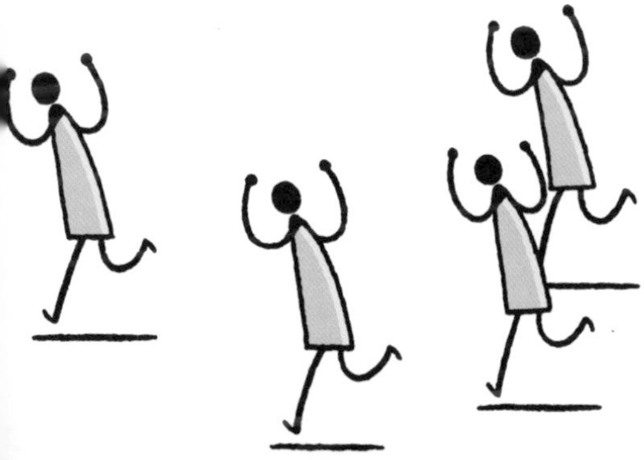

FOR MY GRANDFATHER, DR. DAVID GAULD

CARDS FOR SCIENTISTS FROM THEIR NON-SCIENTIST RELATIONS

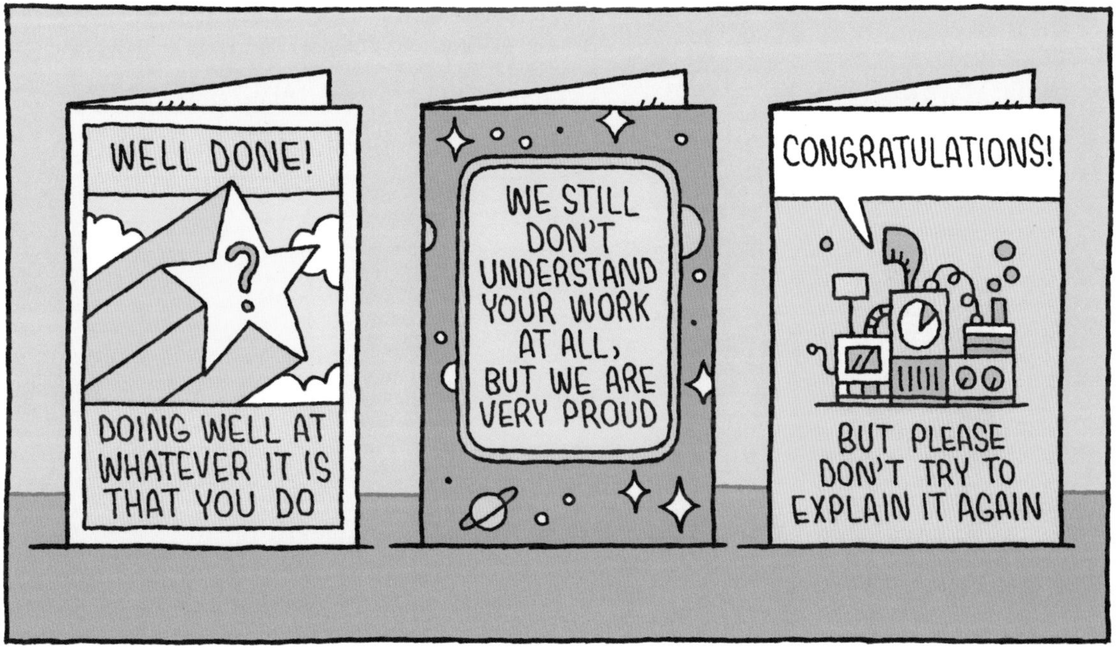
WELL DONE!
DOING WELL AT WHATEVER IT IS THAT YOU DO
WE STILL DON'T UNDERSTAND YOUR WORK AT ALL, BUT WE ARE VERY PROUD
CONGRATULATIONS!
BUT PLEASE DON'T TRY TO EXPLAIN IT AGAIN

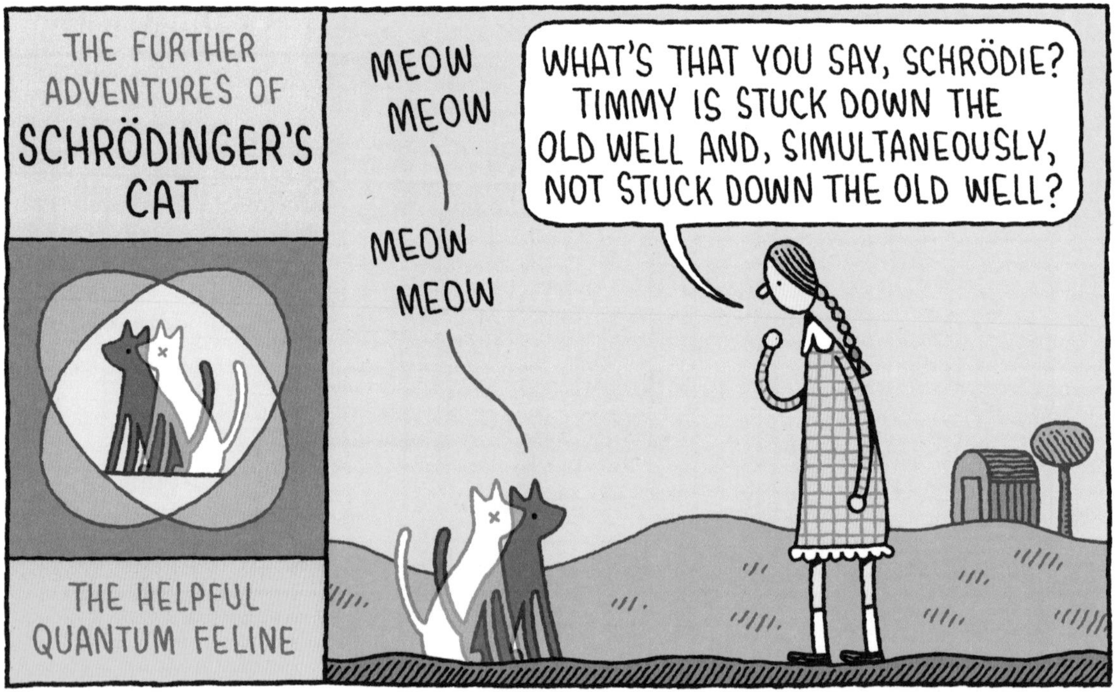
THE FURTHER ADVENTURES OF
SCHRÖDINGER'S CAT
THE HELPFUL QUANTUM FELINE
MEOW MEOW
MEOW MEOW
WHAT'S THAT YOU SAY, SCHRÖDIE? TIMMY IS STUCK DOWN THE OLD WELL AND, SIMULTANEOUSLY, NOT STUCK DOWN THE OLD WELL?

THE UNDISCOVERED SPECIES

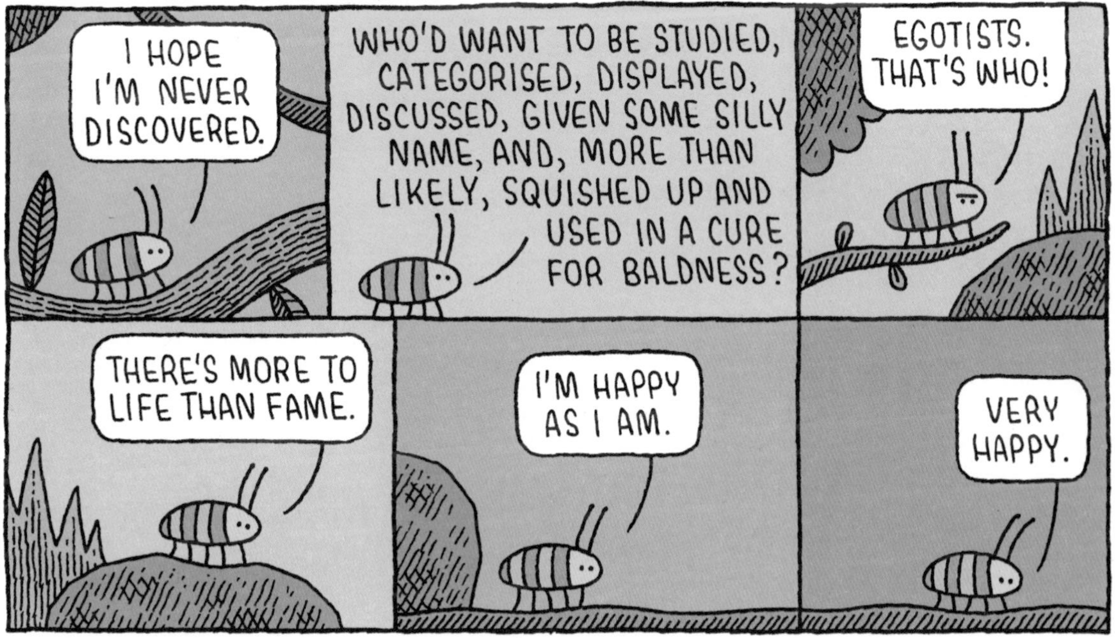
I HOPE I'M NEVER DISCOVERED.
WHO'D WANT TO BE STUDIED, CATEGORISED, DISPLAYED, DISCUSSED, GIVEN SOME SILLY NAME, AND, MORE THAN LIKELY, SQUISHED UP AND USED IN A CURE FOR BALDNESS?
EGOTISTS. THAT'S WHO!
THERE'S MORE TO LIFE THAN FAME.
I'M HAPPY AS I AM.
VERY HAPPY.

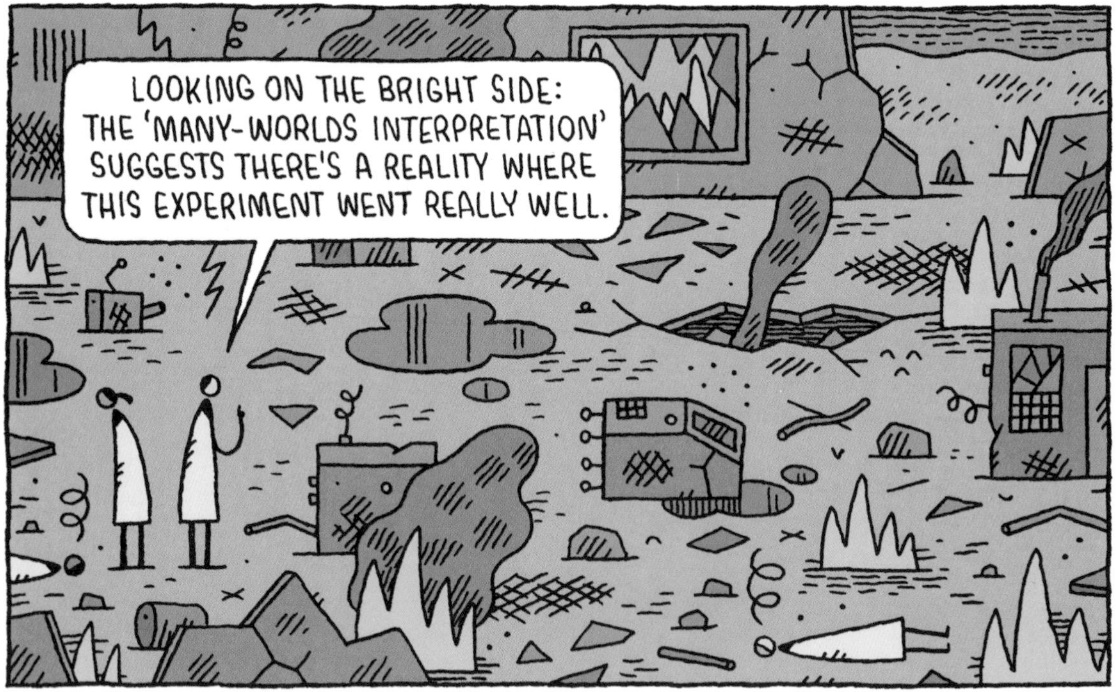
LOOKING ON THE BRIGHT SIDE: THE 'MANY-WORLDS INTERPRETATION' SUGGESTS THERE'S A REALITY WHERE THIS EXPERIMENT WENT REALLY WELL.

THERE'S A GIANT EYE AT THE WINDOW!
NEVER MIND THAT. I'VE SUCCEEDED IN CREATING A PERFECT, TINY REPLICA OF THIS ROOM WITH US IN IT!
THERE'S A GIANT EYE AT THE WINDOW!
NEVER MIND THAT. I'VE SUCCEEDED IN CREATING A PERFECT, TINY...

THE THEORETICAL PARTICLE
HINTED AT
IMAGINED
DESCRIBED
HUNTED FOR
DEBATED
DISPROVED
FORGOTTEN

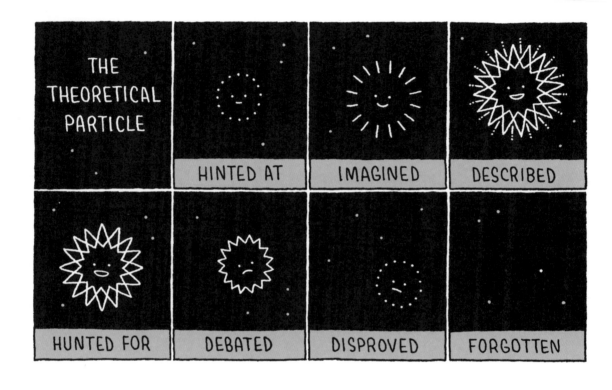

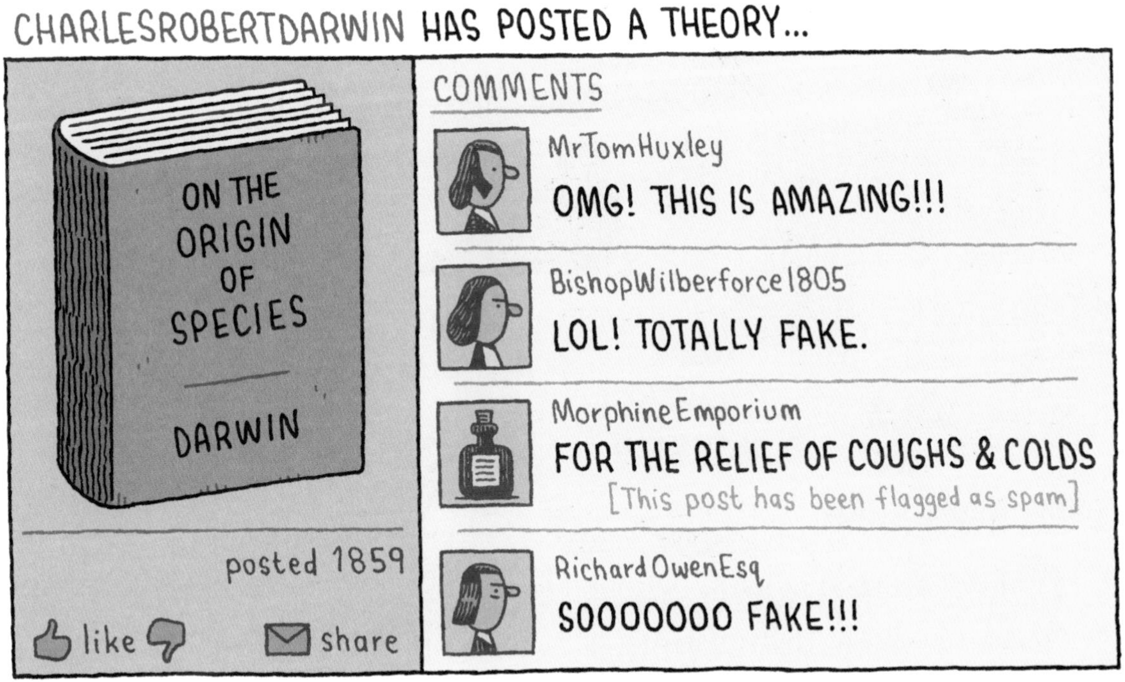

CHARLESROBERTDARWIN HAS POSTED A THEORY...
ON THE ORIGIN OF SPECIES
DARWIN
posted 1859
like
share
COMMENTS
MrTomHuxley
OMG! THIS IS AMAZING!!!
BishopWilberforce1805
LOL! TOTALLY FAKE.
MorphineEmporium
FOR THE RELIEF OF COUGHS & COLDS
[This post has been flagged as spam]
RichardOwenEsq
SOOOOOOO FAKE!!!

THE MELTING ICE HAS REVEALED...

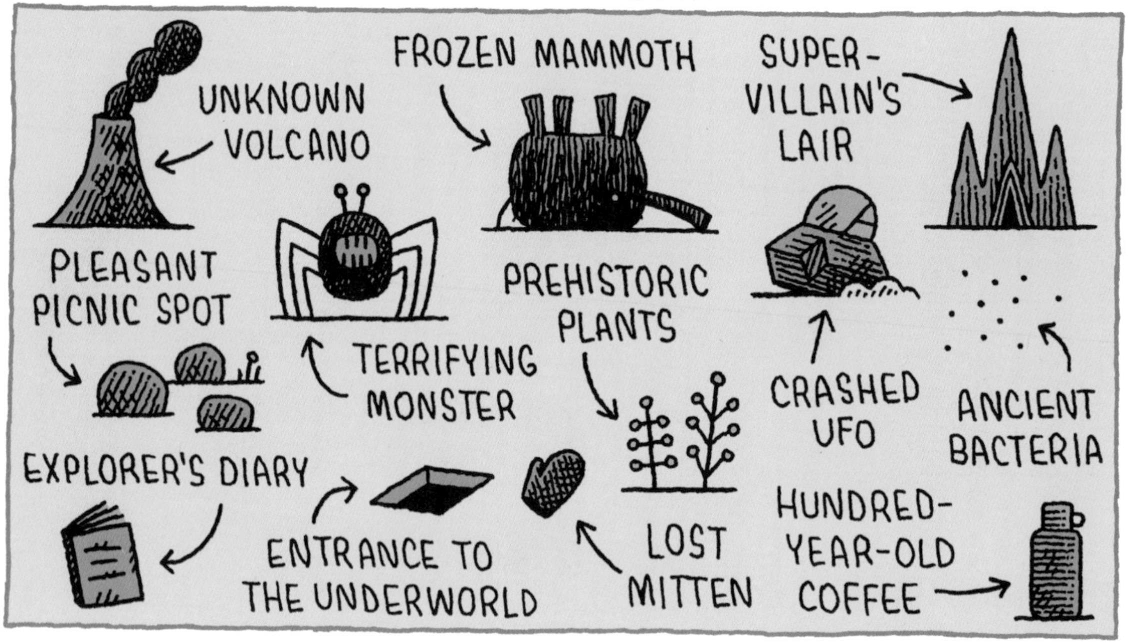
UNKNOWN VOLCANO
FROZEN MAMMOTH
SUPER-VILLAIN'S LAIR
PLEASANT PICNIC SPOT
TERRIFYING MONSTER
PREHISTORIC PLANTS
CRASHED UFO
ANCIENT BACTERIA
EXPLORER'S DIARY
ENTRANCE TO THE UNDERWORLD
LOST MITTEN
HUNDRED-YEAR-OLD COFFEE

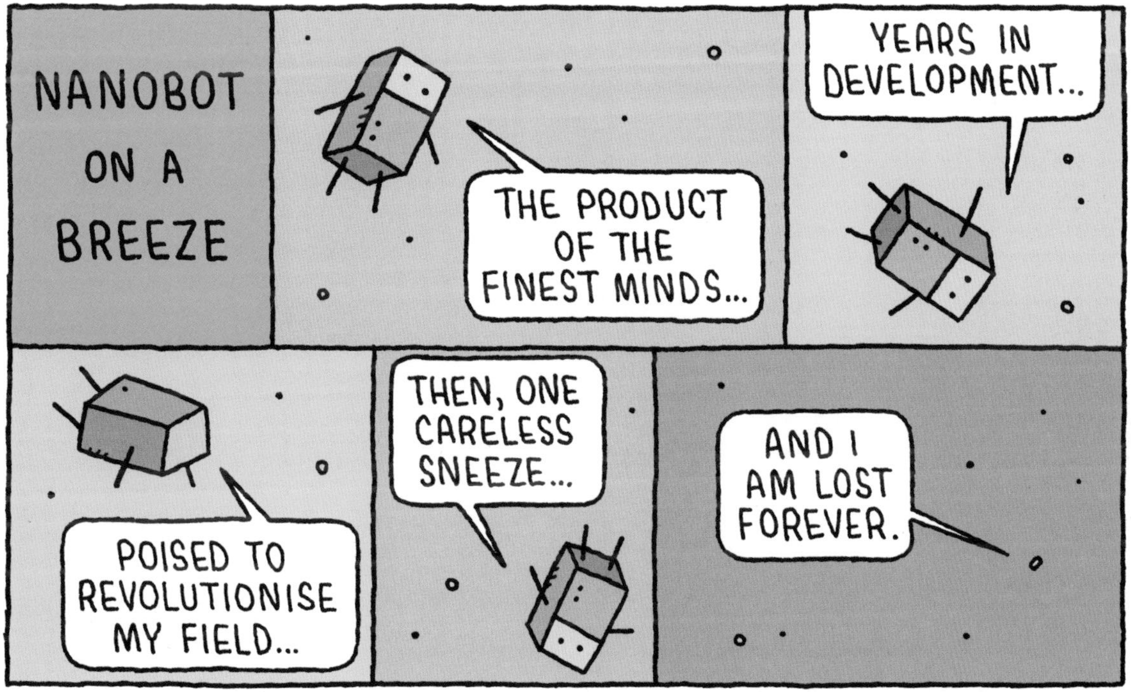
NANOBOT ON A BREEZE
THE PRODUCT OF THE FINEST MINDS...
YEARS IN DEVELOPMENT...
POISED TO REVOLUTIONISE MY FIELD...
THEN, ONE CARELESS SNEEZE...
AND I AM LOST FOREVER.

THE ANNUAL CONFERENCE OF THE SOCIETY OF CANINE OSTEOLOGISTS

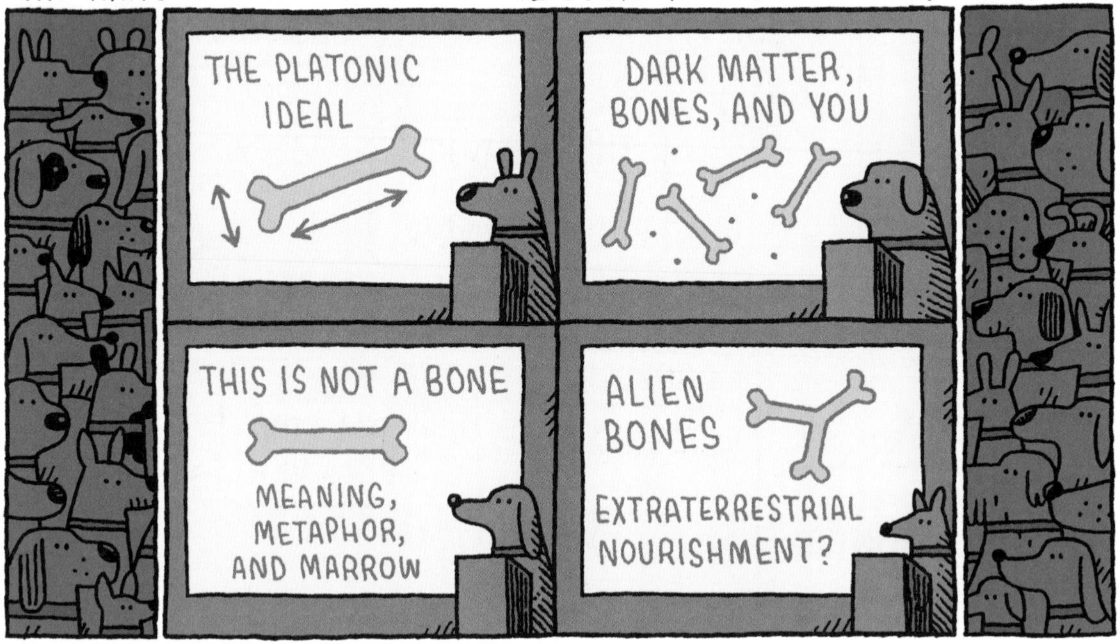
THE PLATONIC IDEAL
DARK MATTER, BONES, AND YOU
THIS IS NOT A BONE
MEANING, METAPHOR, AND MARROW
ALIEN BONES
EXTRATERRESTRIAL NOURISHMENT?

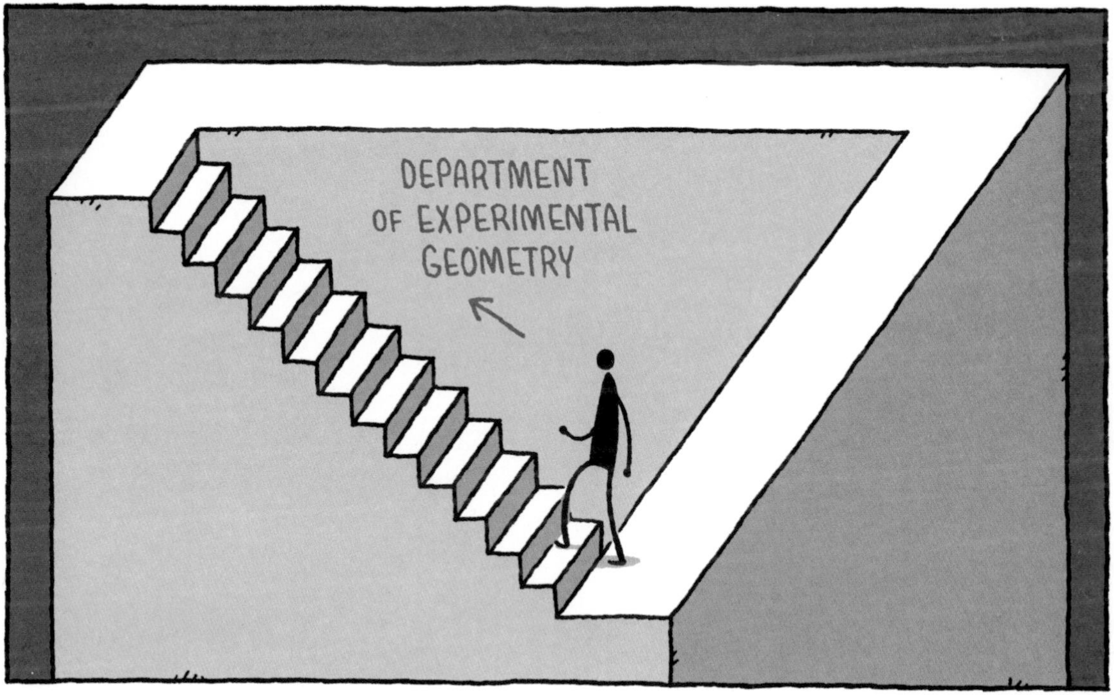
DEPARTMENT
OF EXPERIMENTAL
GEOMETRY

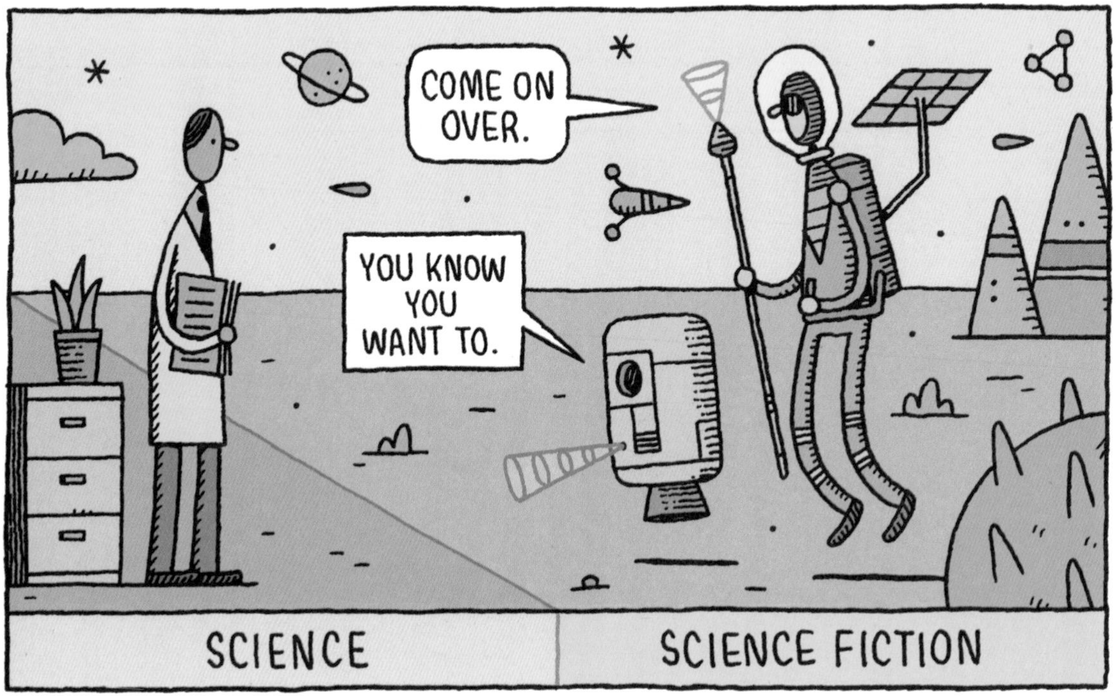
COME ON OVER.
YOU KNOW YOU WANT TO.
SCIENCE
SCIENCE FICTION

DISPLAY CASE 403 'TWO INSECTS PRESERVED IN AMBER'

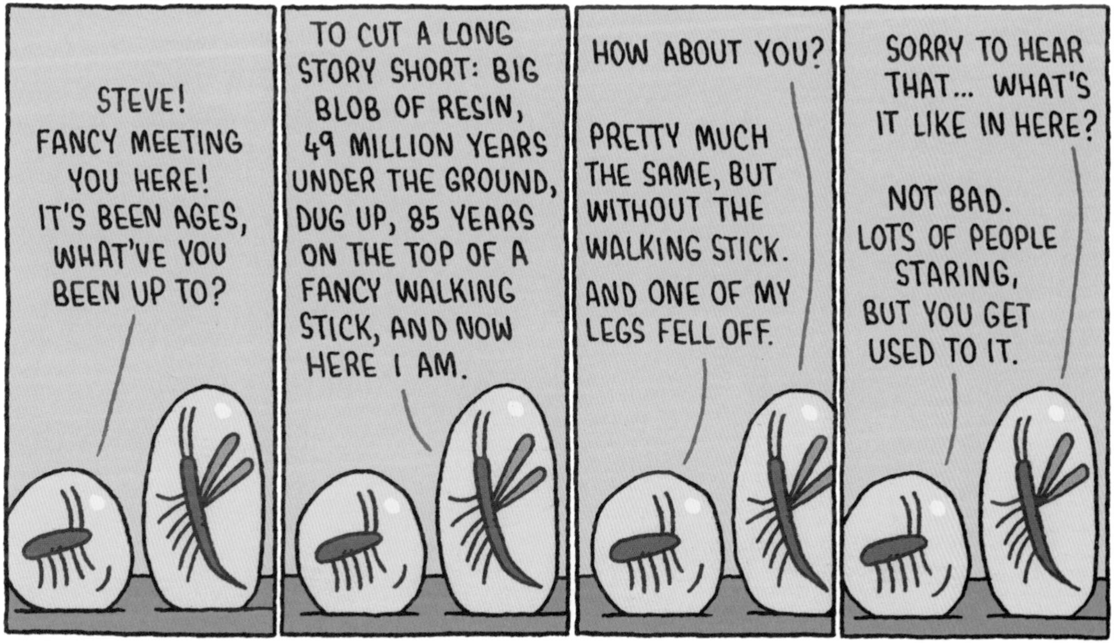
STEVE! FANCY MEETING YOU HERE! IT'S BEEN AGES, WHAT'VE YOU BEEN UP TO?
TO CUT A LONG STORY SHORT: BIG BLOB OF RESIN, 49 MILLION YEARS UNDER THE GROUND, DUG UP, 85 YEARS ON THE TOP OF A FANCY WALKING STICK, AND NOW HERE I AM.
HOW ABOUT YOU?
PRETTY MUCH THE SAME, BUT WITHOUT THE WALKING STICK.
AND ONE OF MY LEGS FELL OFF.
SORRY TO HEAR THAT... WHAT'S IT LIKE IN HERE?
NOT BAD. LOTS OF PEOPLE STARING, BUT YOU GET USED TO IT.

PICTURE BOOK SUGGESTIONS FOR YOUNG BACTERIOLOGISTS

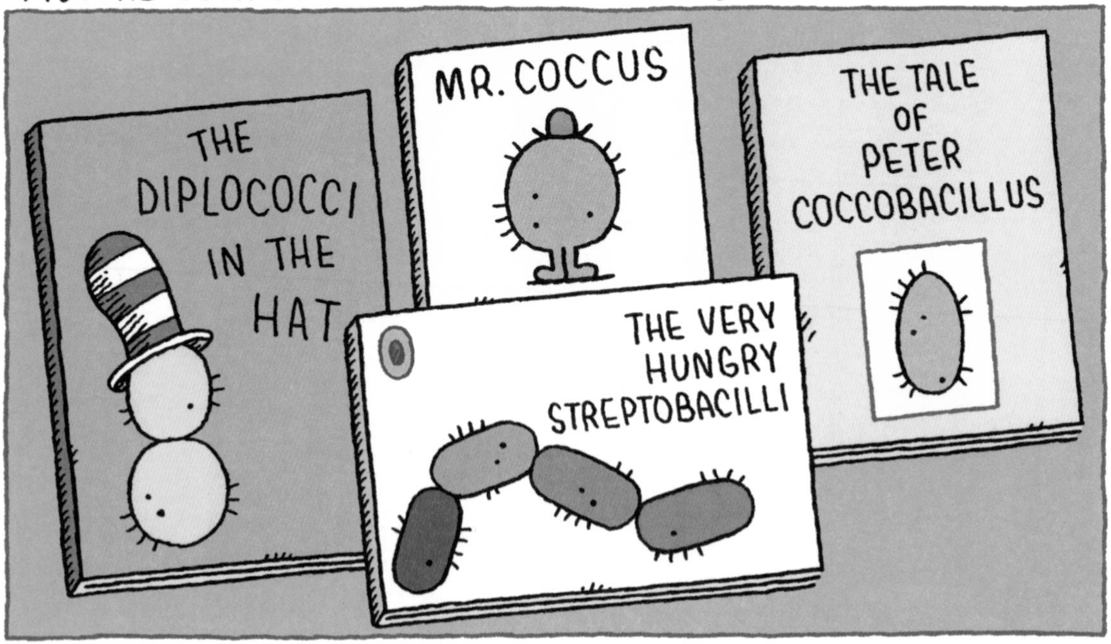
THE DIPLOCOCCI IN THE HAT
MR. COCCUS
THE TALE OF PETER COCCOBACILLUS
THE VERY HUNGRY STREPTOBACILLI

WILLIAM MORRIS PATTERNS UPDATED AND REISSUED

SWEET BRIAR
AND MICRO-BOT

OAK TREE
AND CAM-DROID

MICHAELMAS DAISY
AND FLY-DRONE

PAVLOV'S HOUSEHOLD

THE BELL RINGS.

THE DOG SALIVATES.

THE SCIENTIST RECORDS THIS.

THE DINNER BELL RINGS.

THE SCIENTIST GOES DOWN TO DINNER.

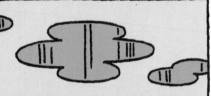

THE MAID WONDERS WHY THERE IS SO MUCH DOG DROOL EVERYWHERE.

THE FUTURE OF THE AUTOMOBILE

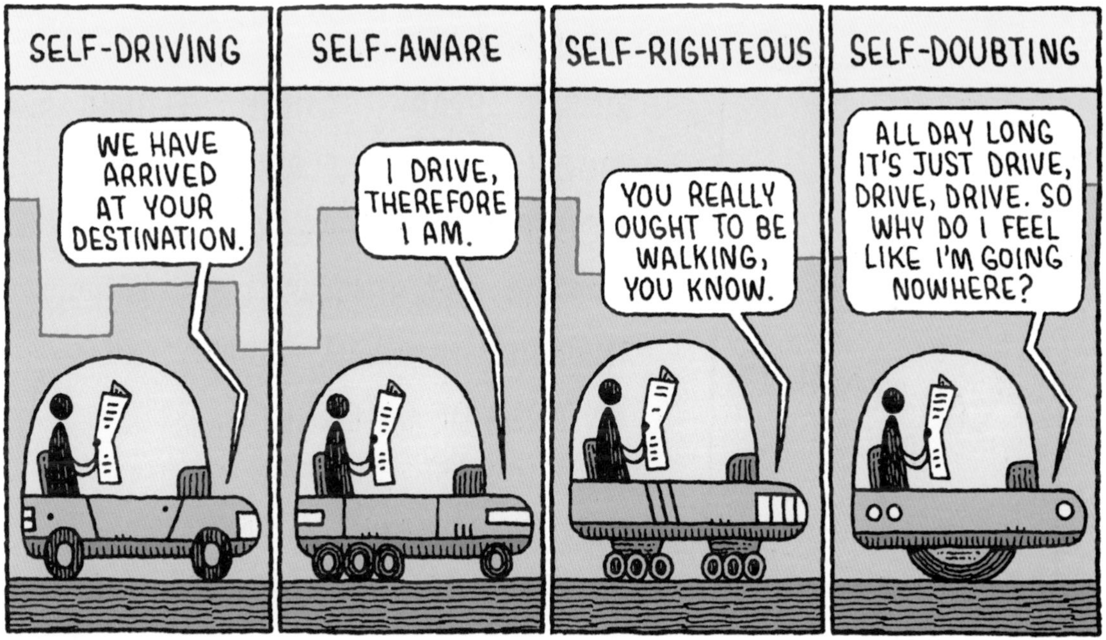
SELF-DRIVING
WE HAVE ARRIVED AT YOUR DESTINATION.
SELF-AWARE
I DRIVE, THEREFORE I AM.
SELF-RIGHTEOUS
YOU REALLY OUGHT TO BE WALKING, YOU KNOW.
SELF-DOUBTING
ALL DAY LONG IT'S JUST DRIVE, DRIVE, DRIVE. SO WHY DO I FEEL LIKE I'M GOING NOWHERE?

POPULAR SCIENCE BESTSELLER TITLE GENERATOR

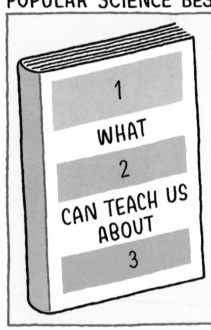

1. A SNAPPY TITLE:

BINGO! SPARK! QUIRK! FLUMP!

DOOZY! WHIZZ! FLASH! ZILCH!

2. A CULTURAL REFERENCE:

PEPPA PIG THE BEATLES GOLF MUESLI

SNAPCHAT BATMAN ZUMBA CHER

3. AN AREA OF SCIENCE:

ASTROPHYSICS QUANTUM MECHANICS

MOLECULAR BIOLOGY CRYSTALLOGRAPHY

NEUROSCIENCE POLYMER CHEMISTRY

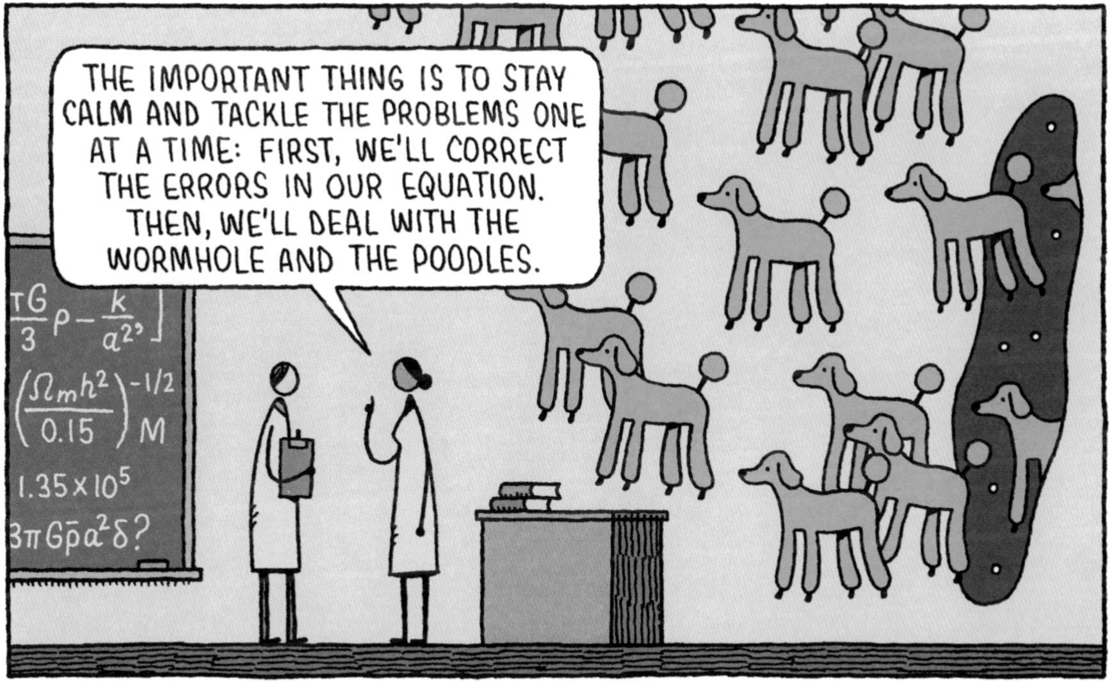
THE IMPORTANT THING IS TO STAY CALM AND TACKLE THE PROBLEMS ONE AT A TIME: FIRST, WE'LL CORRECT THE ERRORS IN OUR EQUATION. THEN, WE'LL DEAL WITH THE WORMHOLE AND THE POODLES.

NEW SIGNS FOR THE SCIENCE PARK

ROBOT
SCHOOL
ZONE

CARAVAN PARK
WITH BIOHAZARD
STORAGE FACILITIES

DEPARTMENT OF
MINDBLOWING
THEORIES

BEWARE OF
LOW-FLYING
DRONES

NUCLEAR-POWERED
HOVER TRUCKS
ONLY

SINISTER
EXPERIMENTS
SECTOR

GIVE WAY TO
ELDERLY
JETPACKERS

CAUTION:
HAZARDOUS
MATHEMATICS

WHAT IS THE SECRET OF YOUR SCIENTIFIC SUCCESS?

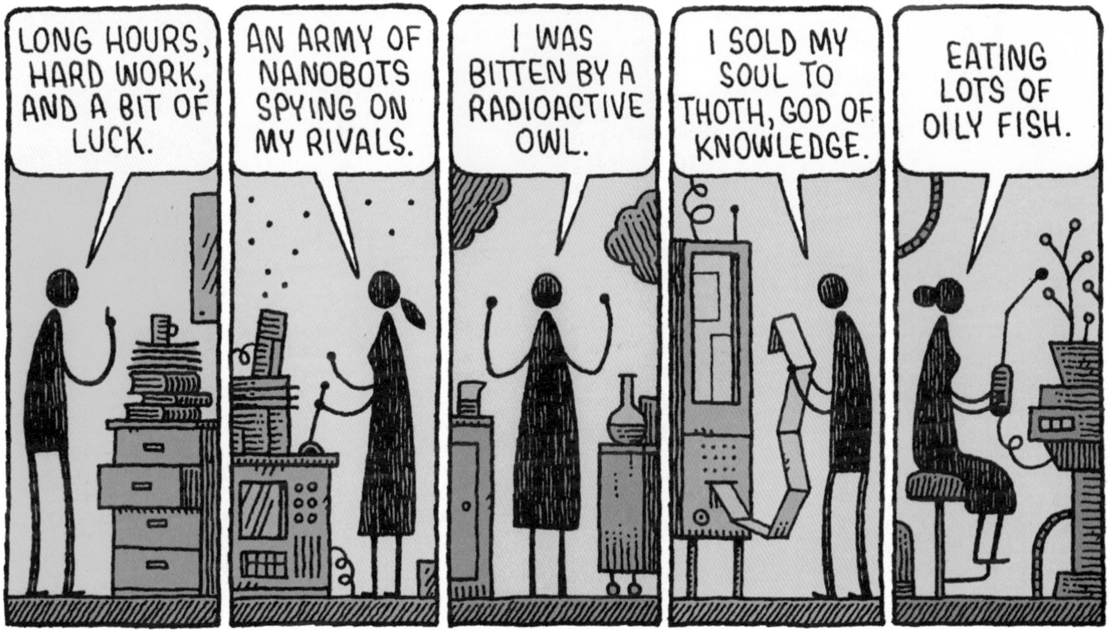
LONG HOURS, HARD WORK, AND A BIT OF LUCK.
AN ARMY OF NANOBOTS SPYING ON MY RIVALS.
I WAS BITTEN BY A RADIOACTIVE OWL.
I SOLD MY SOUL TO THOTH, GOD OF KNOWLEDGE.
EATING LOTS OF OILY FISH.

OUR COMPREHENSIVE ANALYSIS
INCONCLUSIVE RESULT
PROBABLY NOTHING
NOT ENOUGH DATA
GLITCH
HUMAN ERROR
NOISE
OTHER
TOO EARLY TO SAY
MISCALCULATION
UNKNOWN
EQUIPMENT MALFUNCTION
INVALID READING
DON'T KNOW

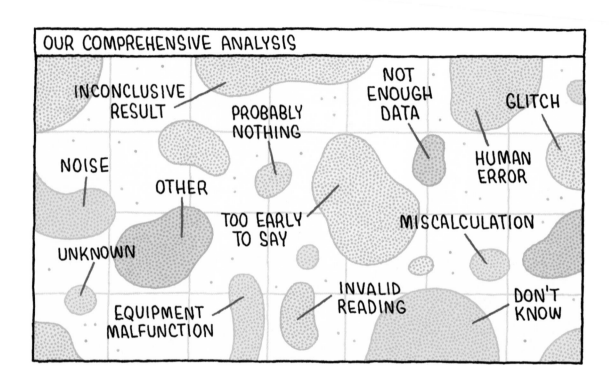

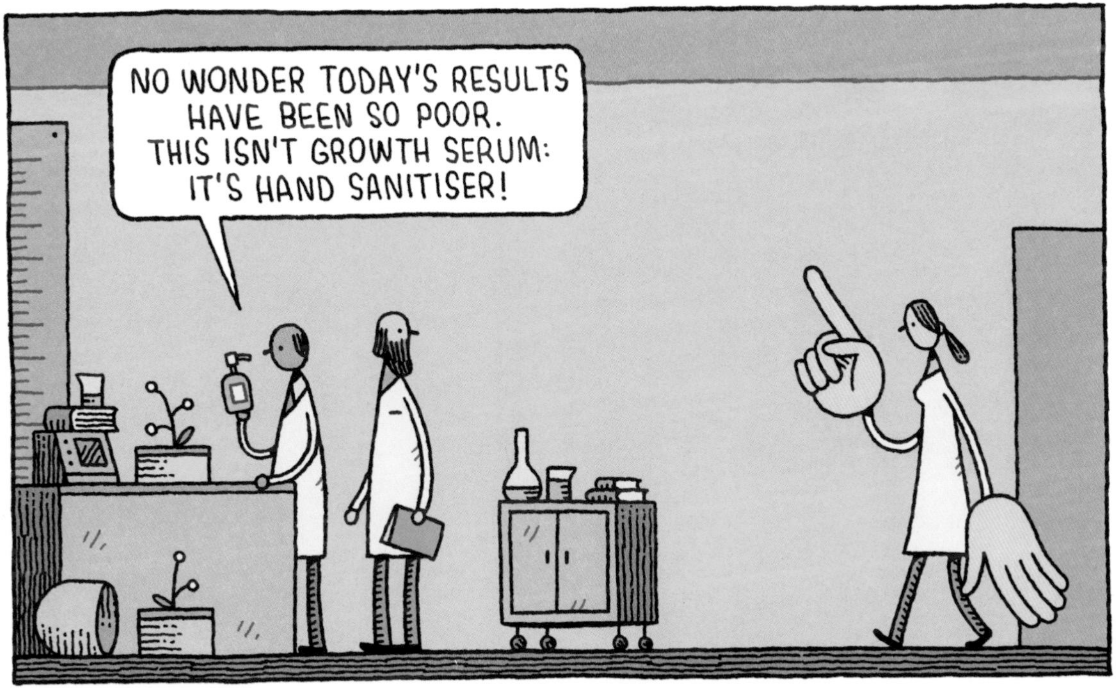
NO WONDER TODAY'S RESULTS HAVE BEEN SO POOR. THIS ISN'T GROWTH SERUM: IT'S HAND SANITISER!

NEW ISSUES OUT NOW
UTOPIAN SCIENCE QUARTERLY
ROBOT SERVANTS
NEW WORLDS
LIVING PAST 200?
JETPACK OR FLYING CAR?
10 AMAZING BREAKTHROUGHS JUST AROUND THE CORNER!
THE JOURNAL OF DYSTOPIAN SCIENCE
KNOW YOUR SUPERBUGS
DIGITAL MELTDOWN
ASTEROID STRIKES
MASS EXTINCTIONS
10 BAD THINGS THAT ARE ONLY GOING TO GET WORSE!

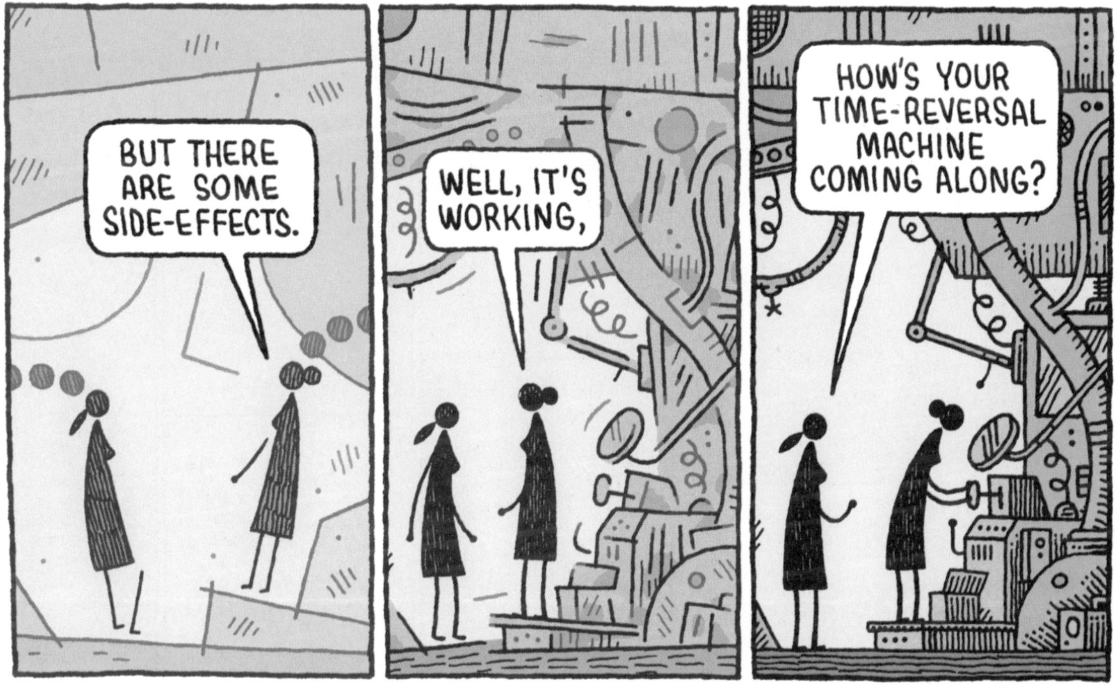
BUT THERE ARE SOME SIDE-EFFECTS.
WELL, IT'S WORKING,
HOW'S YOUR TIME-REVERSAL MACHINE COMING ALONG?

PUZZLE: THE SCIENTIST'S RIVER PROBLEM

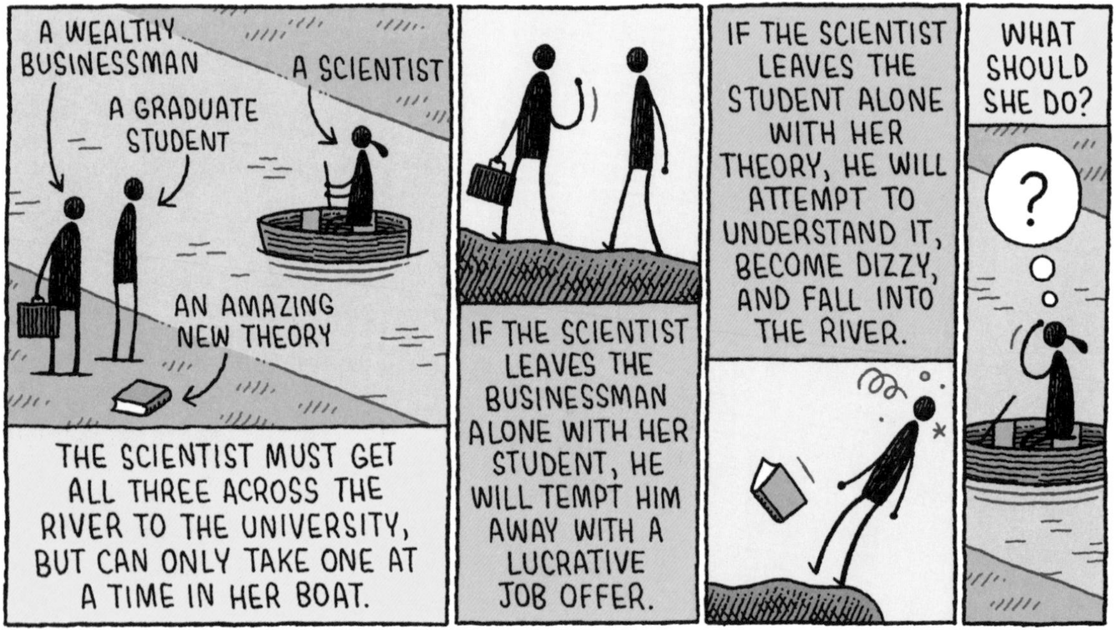
A WEALTHY BUSINESSMAN
A GRADUATE STUDENT
A SCIENTIST
AN AMAZING NEW THEORY
THE SCIENTIST MUST GET ALL THREE ACROSS THE RIVER TO THE UNIVERSITY, BUT CAN ONLY TAKE ONE AT A TIME IN HER BOAT.
IF THE SCIENTIST LEAVES THE BUSINESSMAN ALONE WITH HER STUDENT, HE WILL TEMPT HIM AWAY WITH A LUCRATIVE JOB OFFER.
IF THE SCIENTIST LEAVES THE STUDENT ALONE WITH HER THEORY, HE WILL ATTEMPT TO UNDERSTAND IT, BECOME DIZZY, AND FALL INTO THE RIVER.
WHAT SHOULD SHE DO?
?

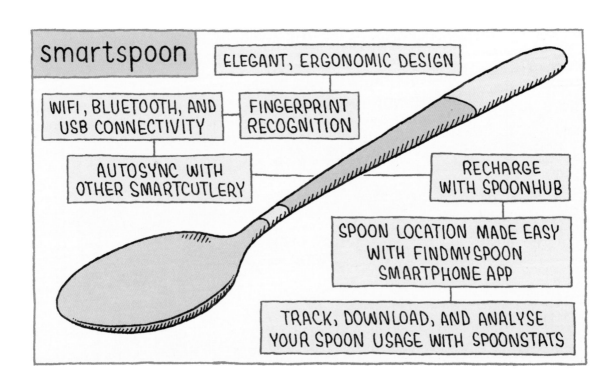

smartspoon

ELEGANT, ERGONOMIC DESIGN

WIFI, BLUETOOTH, AND USB CONNECTIVITY

FINGERPRINT RECOGNITION

AUTOSYNC WITH OTHER SMARTCUTLERY

RECHARGE WITH SPOONHUB

SPOON LOCATION MADE EASY WITH FINDMYSPOON SMARTPHONE APP

TRACK, DOWNLOAD, AND ANALYSE YOUR SPOON USAGE WITH SPOONSTATS

ANOTHER UNSUCCESSFUL TEST OF THE MIND-READING APPARATUS

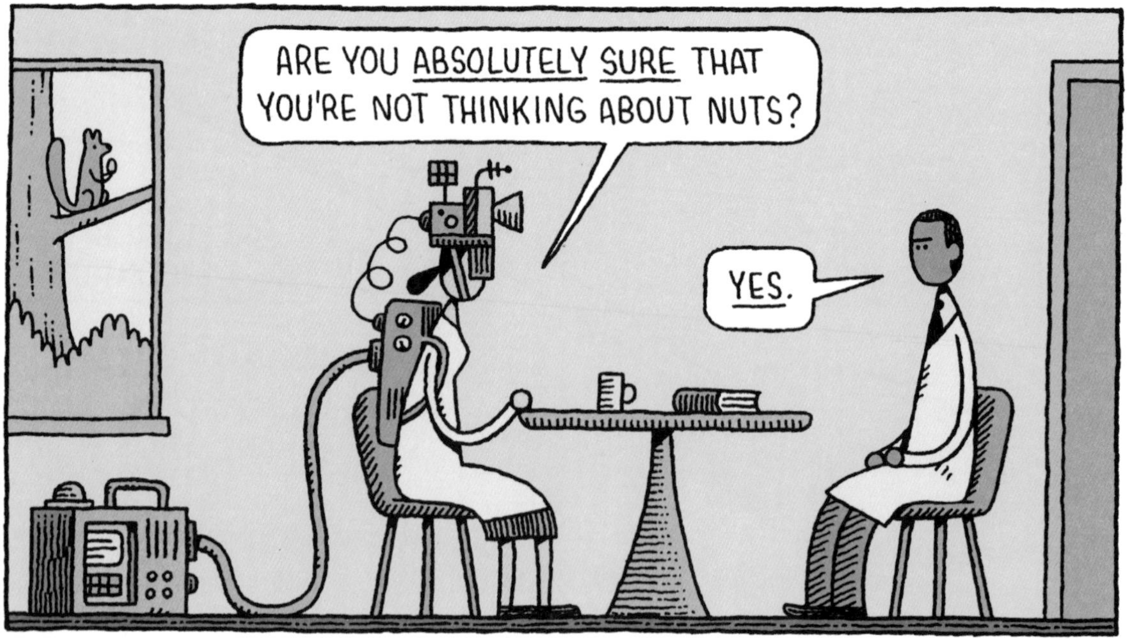
ARE YOU ABSOLUTELY SURE THAT YOU'RE NOT THINKING ABOUT NUTS?
YES.

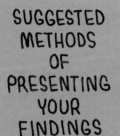
SUGGESTED METHODS OF PRESENTING YOUR FINDINGS

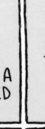
AN ARTICLE IN A PEER-REVIEWED JOURNAL

A POPULAR SCIENCE BESTSELLER

ENGRAVED ON THE WALLS OF A SECRET CHAMBER

A TRANSMISSION BEAMED TO OUR ALIEN MASTERS

A BROADWAY MUSICAL

WHISPERED INTO A HOLE IN AN ENCHANTED OAK

AN INTERNET MEME INVOLVING CATS

#ALCHEMISTS

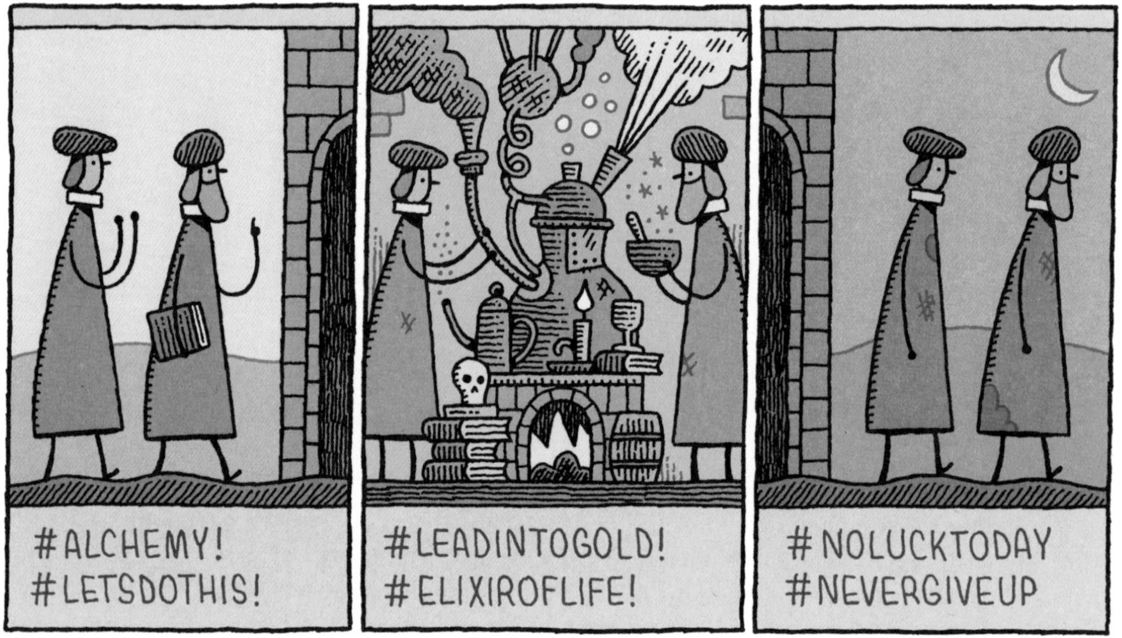
#ALCHEMY!
#LETSDOTHIS!
#LEADINTOGOLD!
#ELIXIROFLIFE!
#NOLUCKTODAY
#NEVERGIVEUP

THE THREE LITTLE SCIENTISTS AND THE BIG BAD WOLF

The big bad wolf came to the first little scientist's house and tried to blow it down. But the house was built of graphene, so was much too strong.

The second little scientist had built his house of ceramic meta-materials. Once again, the big bad wolf tried and failed to blow the house down.

The third little scientist had built his house of nano-engineered concrete. The big bad wolf blew and blew until he fell exhausted to the ground.

The scientists tagged the wolf, released him back into the wild, and began a study of his habitat and behaviour.

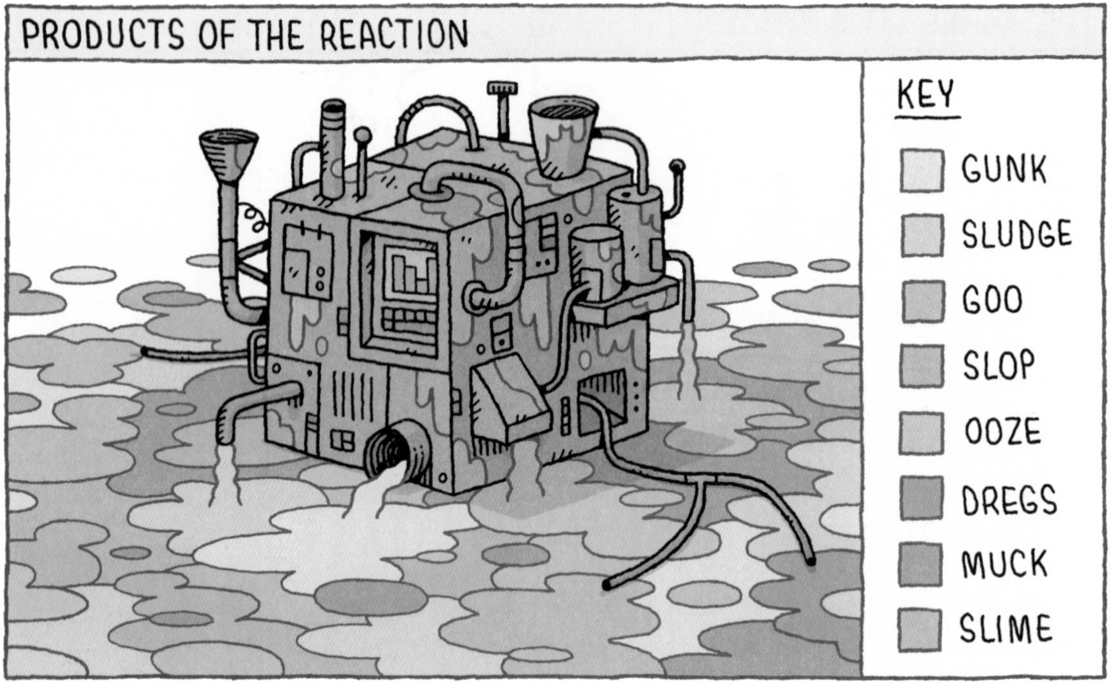
PRODUCTS OF THE REACTION
KEY
GUNK
SLUDGE
GOO
SLOP
OOZE
DREGS
MUCK
SLIME

THE ASTEROID AND THE COMET SECRETLY HATE EACH OTHER

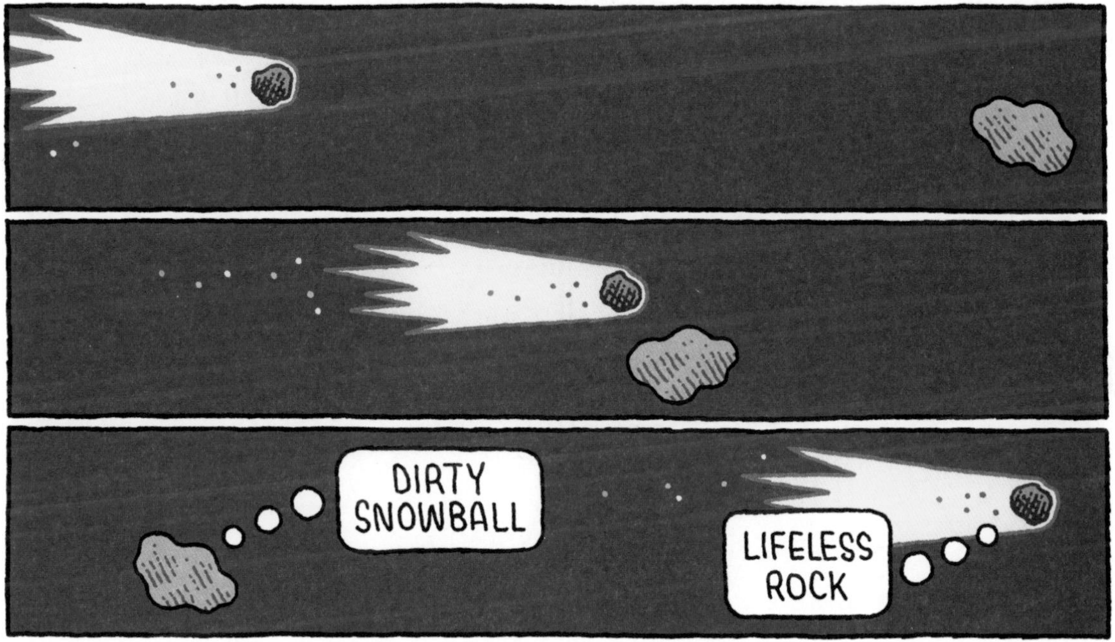
DIRTY SNOWBALL
LIFELESS ROCK

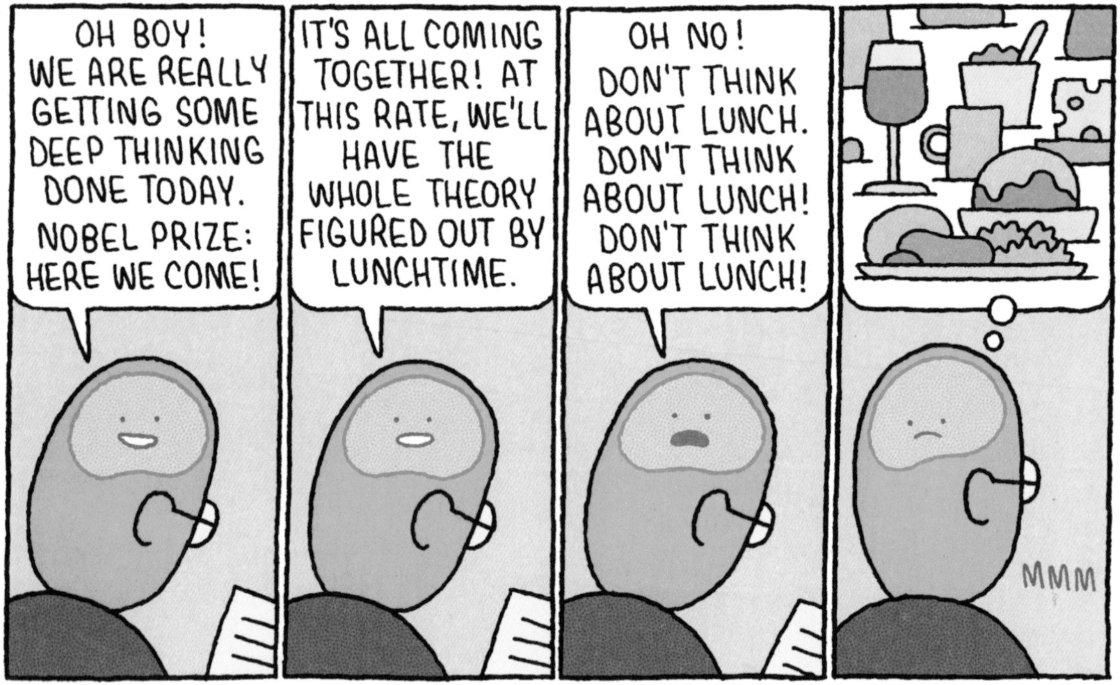

OH BOY! WE ARE REALLY GETTING SOME DEEP THINKING DONE TODAY. NOBEL PRIZE: HERE WE COME!
IT'S ALL COMING TOGETHER! AT THIS RATE, WE'LL HAVE THE WHOLE THEORY FIGURED OUT BY LUNCHTIME.
OH NO! DON'T THINK ABOUT LUNCH. DON'T THINK ABOUT LUNCH! DON'T THINK ABOUT LUNCH!
MMM

fig.53: DROPPINGS COLLECTED IN AN ENCHANTED WOOD

1. GOBLIN

2. FAIRY

3. TROLL

4. CENTAUR

5. ELF

6. GIANT

7. HOBBIT

8. DRAGON

WAITER! WAITER!
THERE'S A FLY IN MY SOUP!
SIR, THIS IS AN ERUDITE SCIENCE CARTOON! WE CAN'T HAVE FLY/SOUP HUMOUR IN HERE. I'M AFRAID YOU'LL HAVE TO LEAVE.
WAIT! I AM A WORLD-FAMOUS ENTOMOLOGIST AND THIS IS AN INCREDIBLY RARE SPECIES OF FLY!
BUT WHAT'S IT DOING IN MY SOUP?
LOOKS LIKE BACKSTROKE!

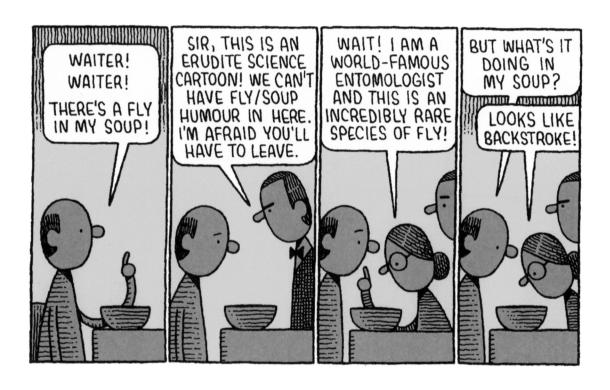

WHAT ARE YOU DOING IN THE WILDERNESS?

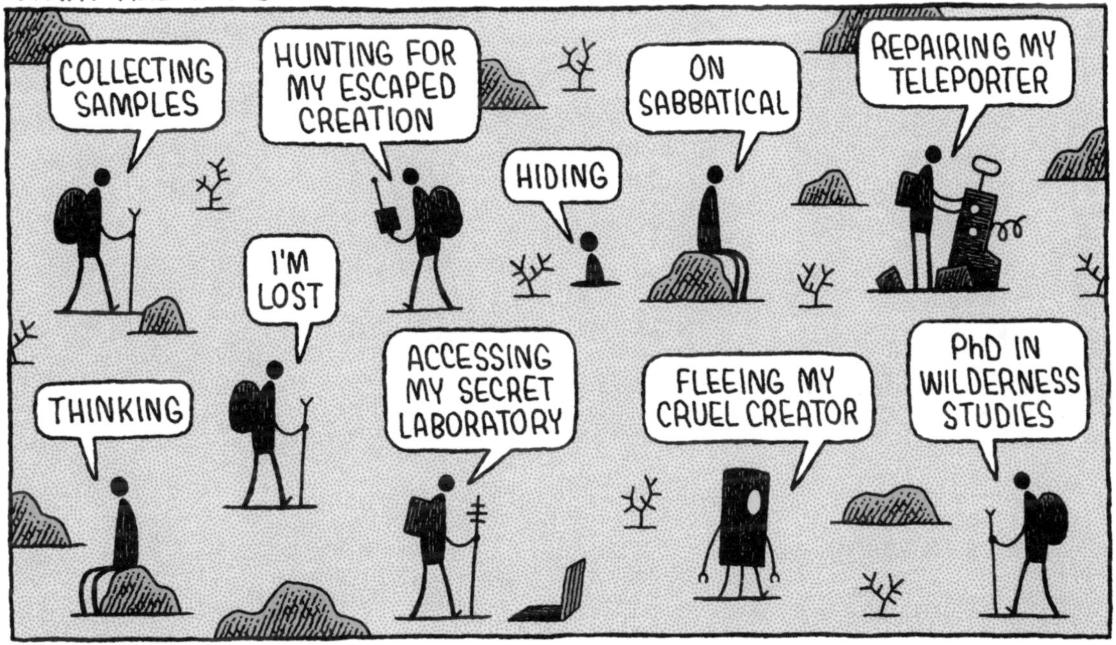
COLLECTING SAMPLES
HUNTING FOR MY ESCAPED CREATION
HIDING
ON SABBATICAL
REPAIRING MY TELEPORTER
I'M LOST
THINKING
ACCESSING MY SECRET LABORATORY
FLEEING MY CRUEL CREATOR
PhD IN WILDERNESS STUDIES

I'M ALL FOR INNOVATION AND INTEGRATION, JULIA. I JUST WONDER IF WE SHOULD CONSIDER A SEPARATE SYSTEM FOR HOT DRINKS.
TEA
FILTER COFFEE
VENT TOXIC GASES
FIRE LASERS
CAPPUCCINO
LAUNCH ROCKET
OPEN ALL CAGES
SYSTEM RESET
INSERT FUEL RODS
RELEASE VIRUS
HOT CHOCOLATE
SELF-DESTRUCT

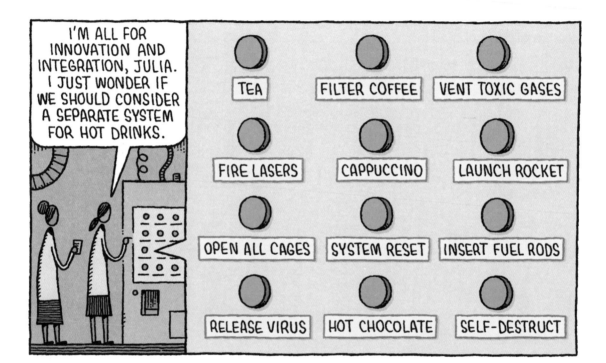

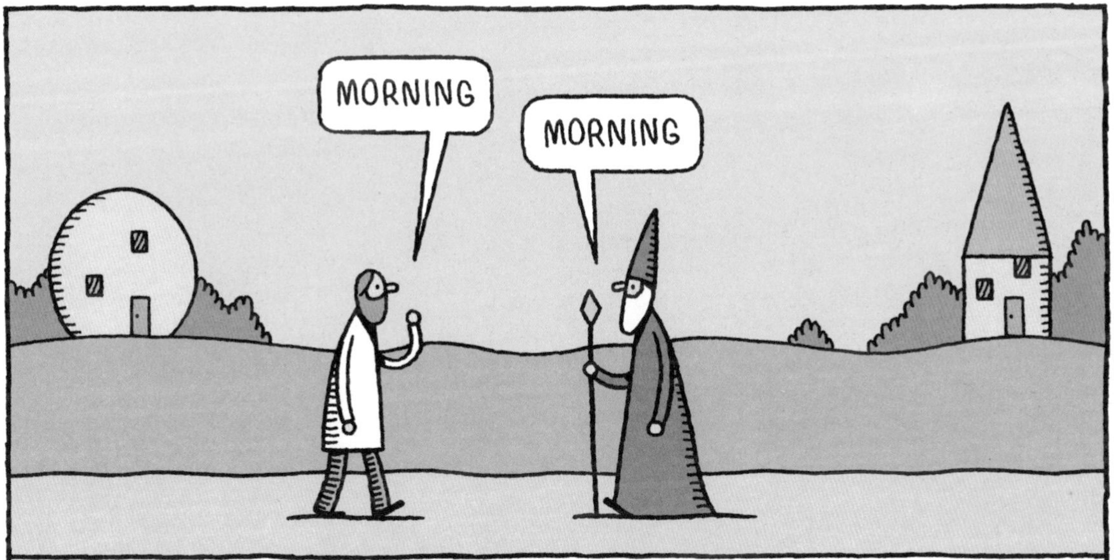
MORNING
MORNING

THE SCIENTIST AND THE WIZARD ARE NEIGHBOURS. THEY GET ALONG WELL, BUT AVOID TALKING ABOUT WORK AS IT ONLY RESULTS IN AN ARGUMENT.

SCIENCE GANG TATTOOS

A
HELL'S ANTHROPOLOGISTS
S·G·P
SOUTH SIDE GEOLOGY POSSE
CCC
CRAZY CHEMISTRY CREW
B B
BOTANY BOYZ
WEST SIDE MATHS BANDIDOS
PARTICLE-PHYSICS SHE-DEVILS
UPTOWN GENETICS MOB

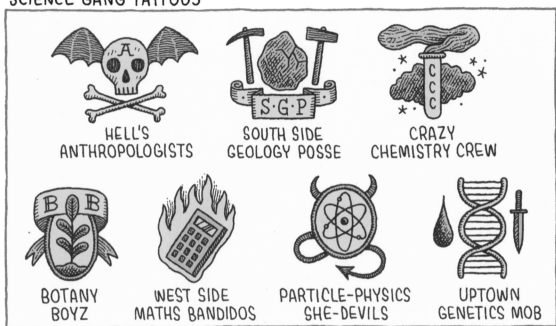

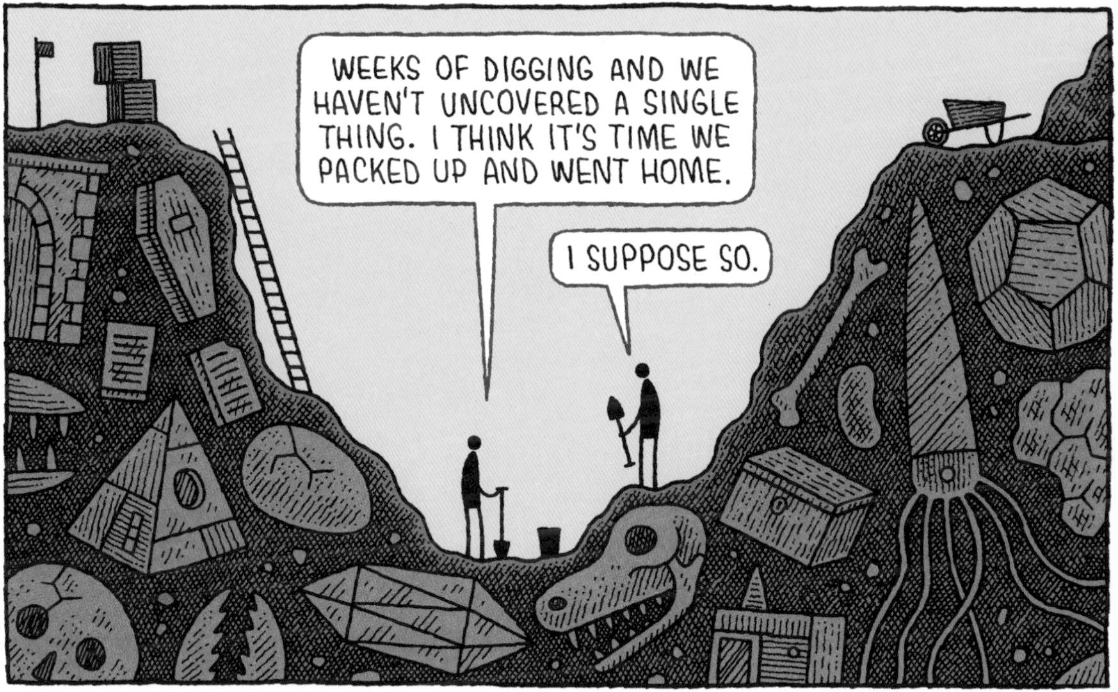
WEEKS OF DIGGING AND WE HAVEN'T UNCOVERED A SINGLE THING. I THINK IT'S TIME WE PACKED UP AND WENT HOME.
I SUPPOSE SO.

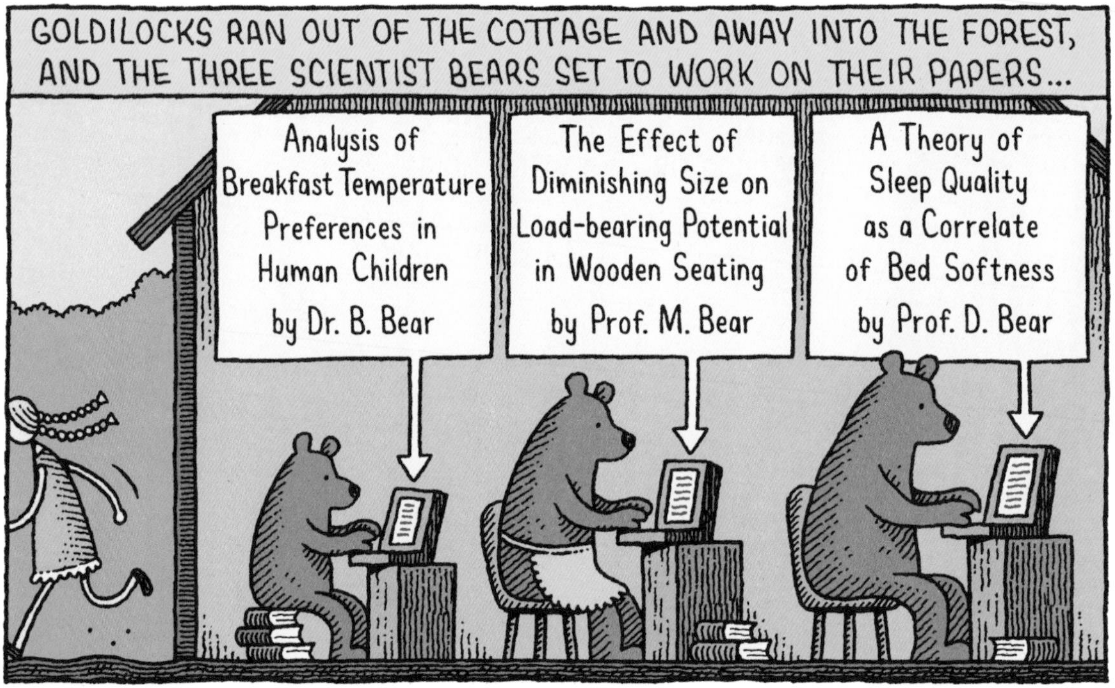

GOLDILOCKS RAN OUT OF THE COTTAGE AND AWAY INTO THE FOREST, AND THE THREE SCIENTIST BEARS SET TO WORK ON THEIR PAPERS...
Analysis of Breakfast Temperature Preferences in Human Children by Dr. B. Bear
The Effect of Diminishing Size on Load-bearing Potential in Wooden Seating by Prof. M. Bear
A Theory of Sleep Quality as a Correlate of Bed Softness by Prof. D. Bear

MY SELF-MINIATURIZATION EXPERIMENT WAS A COMPLETE SUCCESS!!
SO WAS MY ENORMOUS COFFEE CUP EXPERIMENT!

HOLY RELICS OF VENERATED SCIENTISTS

PIPS FROM THE APPLE THAT INSPIRED ISAAC NEWTON.

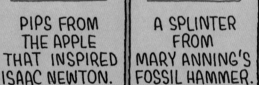

A SPLINTER FROM MARY ANNING'S FOSSIL HAMMER.

A VIAL OF MILK PASTEURISED BY LOUIS PASTEUR HIMSELF.

A SCRAP OF ALBERT EINSTEIN'S TWEED JACKET.

CURIOSITY ROVER

GENEROSITY ROVER

FEROCITY ROVER

VELOCITY ROVER

MONSTROSITY ROVER

POMPOSITY ROVER

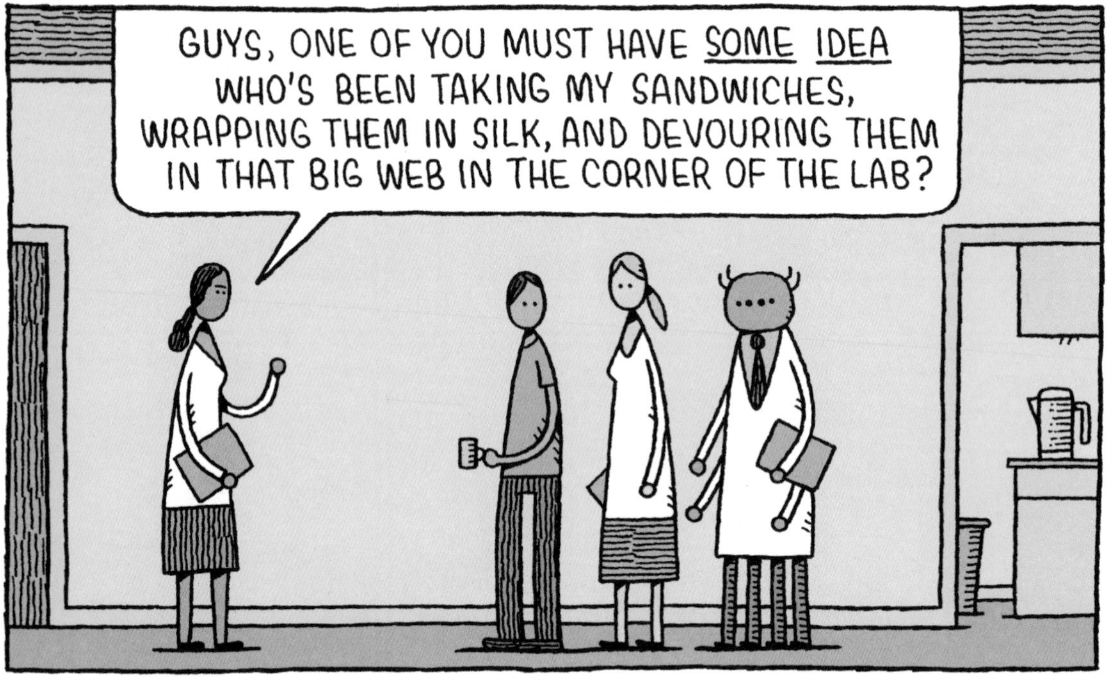
GUYS, ONE OF YOU MUST HAVE SOME IDEA WHO'S BEEN TAKING MY SANDWICHES, WRAPPING THEM IN SILK, AND DEVOURING THEM IN THAT BIG WEB IN THE CORNER OF THE LAB?

LOCAL PUBS FOR SCIENTISTS

THE KING'S PRESERVED HEAD

THE OLDE TRILOBITE

THE LAB-GROWN SWAN

THE ZOOLOGIST AND DRAGON

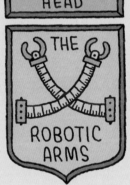

THE ROBOTIC ARMS

THE THEORETICAL TANKARD

THE STRANGE QUARK INN

PROPOSED ADDITIONS TO THE INTERNATIONAL SPACE STATION
MICROBREWERY
SPACE PRISON
COFFEE SHOP
HOLODECK
TELEPORTER
SPA
FOLLY
MONKEY HOUSE
WATERSLIDE
BILLIARD ROOM
ALIEN HATCHERY
YOUTH HOSTEL

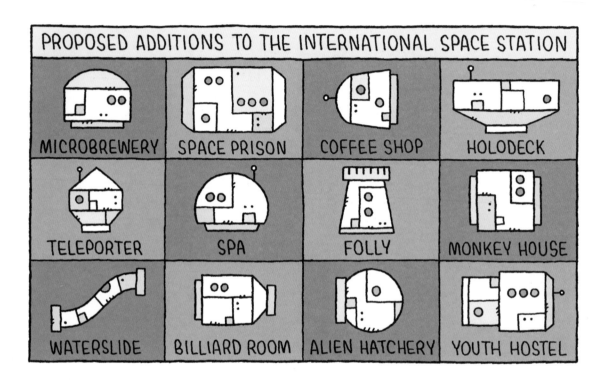

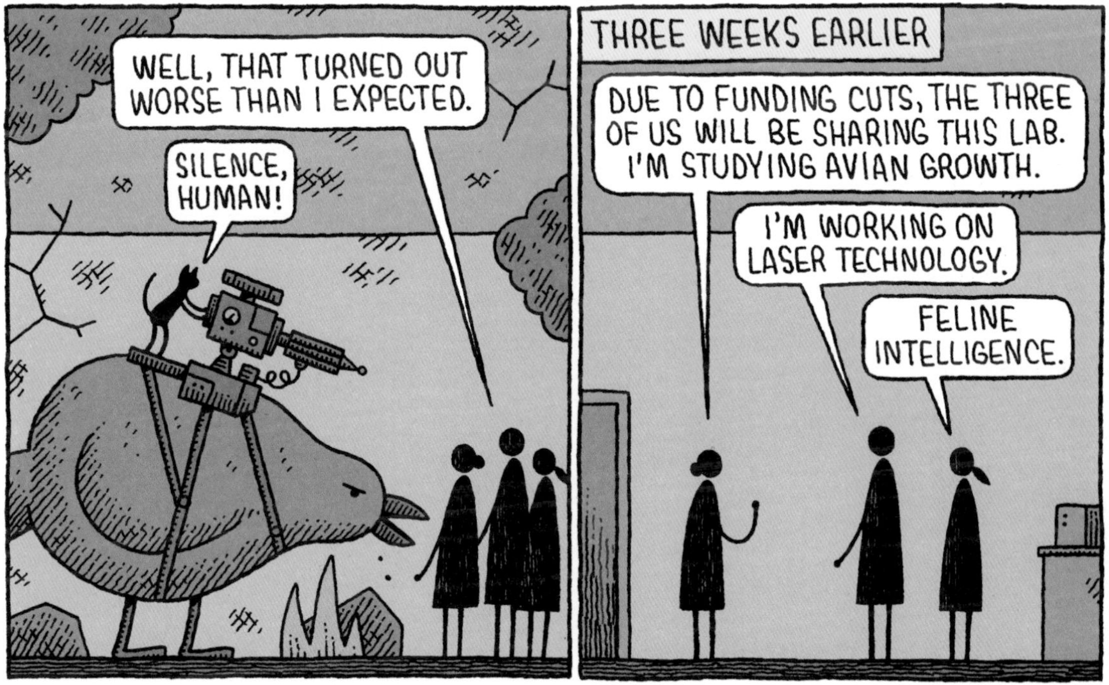

WELL, THAT TURNED OUT WORSE THAN I EXPECTED.
SILENCE, HUMAN!
THREE WEEKS EARLIER
DUE TO FUNDING CUTS, THE THREE OF US WILL BE SHARING THIS LAB. I'M STUDYING AVIAN GROWTH.
I'M WORKING ON LASER TECHNOLOGY.
FELINE INTELLIGENCE.

EVENING CLASSES AT THE DEPARTMENT OF EVIL SCIENCES

MONDAYS

BASIC
NECROMANCY FOR
UNDERGRADUATES

TUESDAYS

DROP-IN
MIND CONTROL
SEMINAR

WEDNESDAYS

MONSTROSITIES AND
ABOMINATIONS
WORKSHOP

THURSDAYS

CREATING SECRET
LABORATORIES
AND LAIRS

FRIDAYS

DEATH RAYS AND
DOOMSDAY MACHINES
FOR BEGINNERS

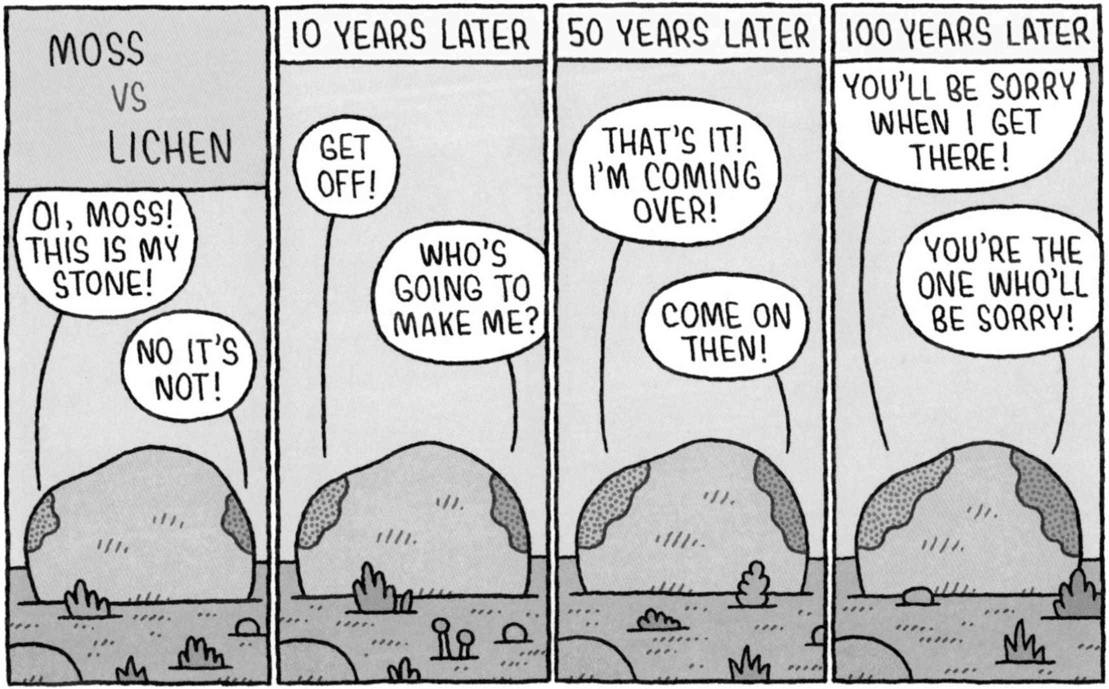
MOSS VS LICHEN
OI, MOSS! THIS IS MY STONE!
NO IT'S NOT!
10 YEARS LATER
GET OFF!
WHO'S GOING TO MAKE ME?
50 YEARS LATER
THAT'S IT! I'M COMING OVER!
COME ON THEN!
100 YEARS LATER
YOU'LL BE SORRY WHEN I GET THERE!
YOU'RE THE ONE WHO'LL BE SORRY!

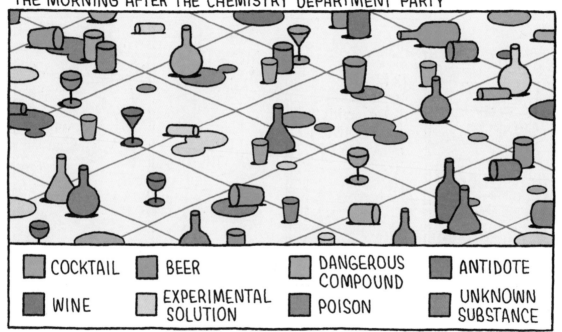

THE MORNING AFTER THE CHEMISTRY DEPARTMENT PARTY

COCKTAIL
WINE
BEER
EXPERIMENTAL SOLUTION
DANGEROUS COMPOUND
POISON
ANTIDOTE
UNKNOWN SUBSTANCE

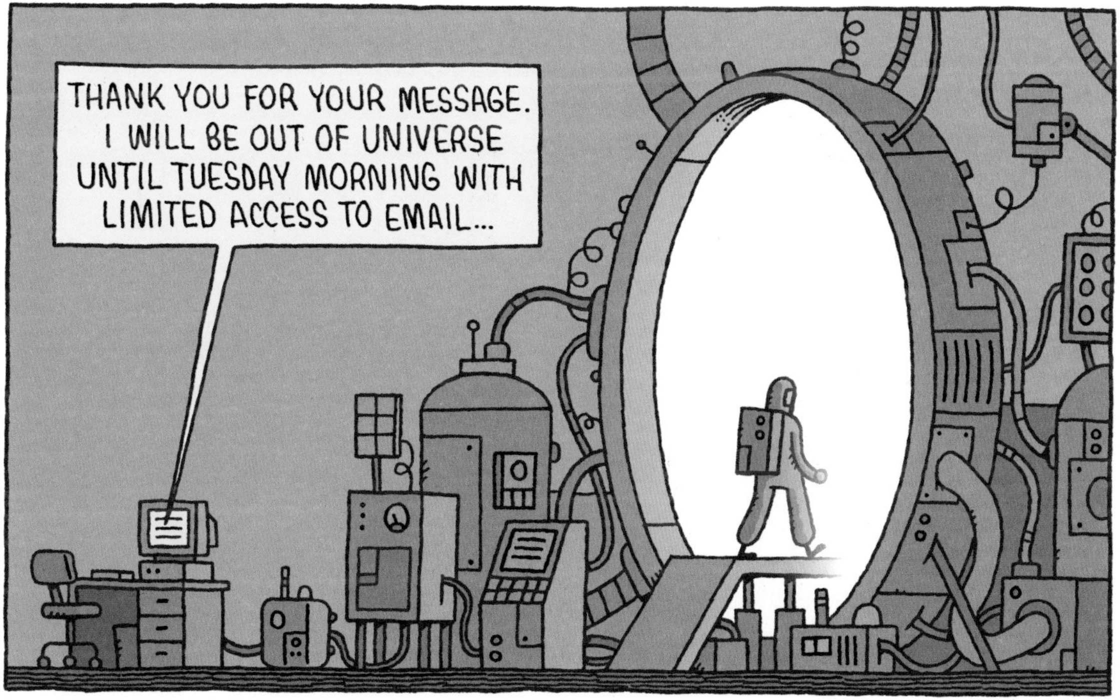
THANK YOU FOR YOUR MESSAGE. I WILL BE OUT OF UNIVERSE UNTIL TUESDAY MORNING WITH LIMITED ACCESS TO EMAIL...

SCIENTISTS
COSMOLOGIST
ENTOMOLOGIST
PHYSICICIST
CHEMIST
PALEONTOLOGIST
BOTANIST
GEOLOGIST
NOT SCIENTISTS
TOURIST
TELEVANGELIST
CUBIST
DUELLIST
TOBACCONIST
TROMBONIST
UNICYCLIST

ANGRY PARTICLE in 'STATES OF MATTER'
TRAPPED IN A PRISON OF OAFS!
SOLID
AWASH IN A MORASS OF IDIOCY!
LIQUID
ADRIFT IN A CLOUD OF DOLTS!
GAS
LOST IN A CHAOTIC SEA OF FOOLS!
PLASMA

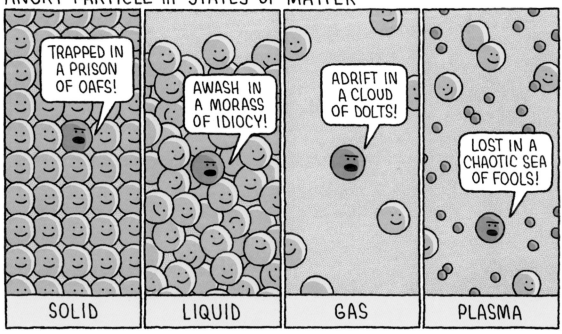

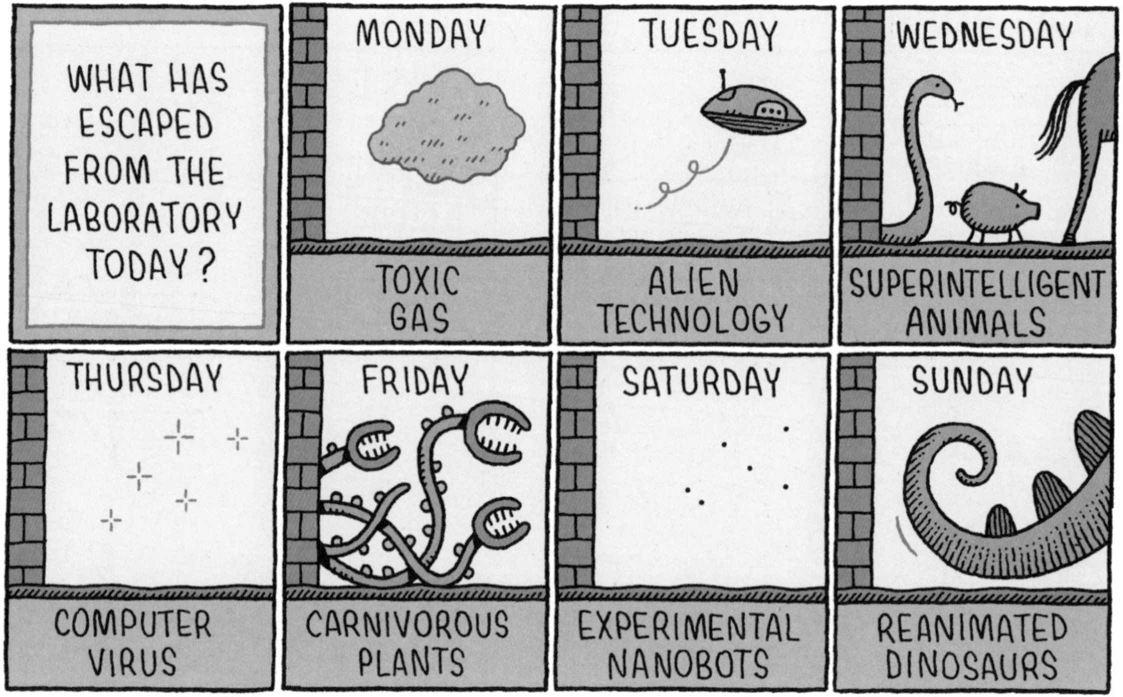
WHAT HAS ESCAPED FROM THE LABORATORY TODAY?
MONDAY
TOXIC GAS
TUESDAY
ALIEN TECHNOLOGY
WEDNESDAY
SUPERINTELLIGENT ANIMALS
THURSDAY
COMPUTER VIRUS
FRIDAY
CARNIVOROUS PLANTS
SATURDAY
EXPERIMENTAL NANOBOTS
SUNDAY
REANIMATED DINOSAURS

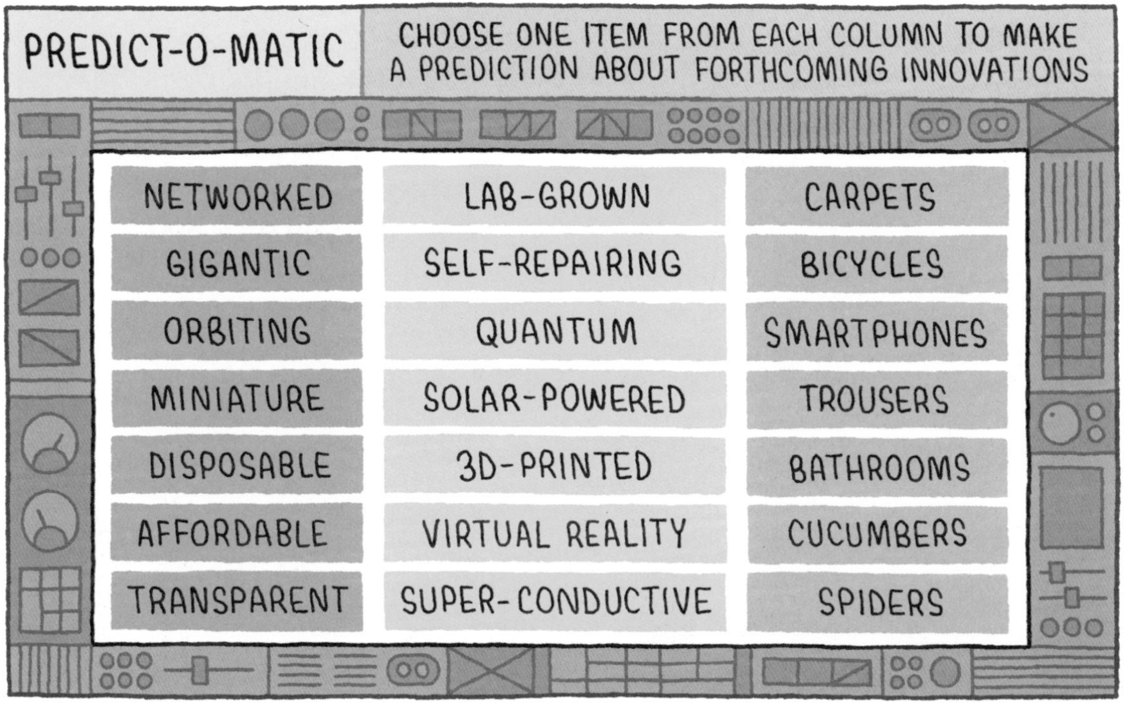
PREDICT-O-MATIC
CHOOSE ONE ITEM FROM EACH COLUMN TO MAKE A PREDICTION ABOUT FORTHCOMING INNOVATIONS
NETWORKED
GIGANTIC
ORBITING
MINIATURE
DISPOSABLE
AFFORDABLE
TRANSPARENT
LAB-GROWN
SELF-REPAIRING
QUANTUM
SOLAR-POWERED
3D-PRINTED
VIRTUAL REALITY
SUPER-CONDUCTIVE
CARPETS
BICYCLES
SMARTPHONES
TROUSERS
BATHROOMS
CUCUMBERS
SPIDERS

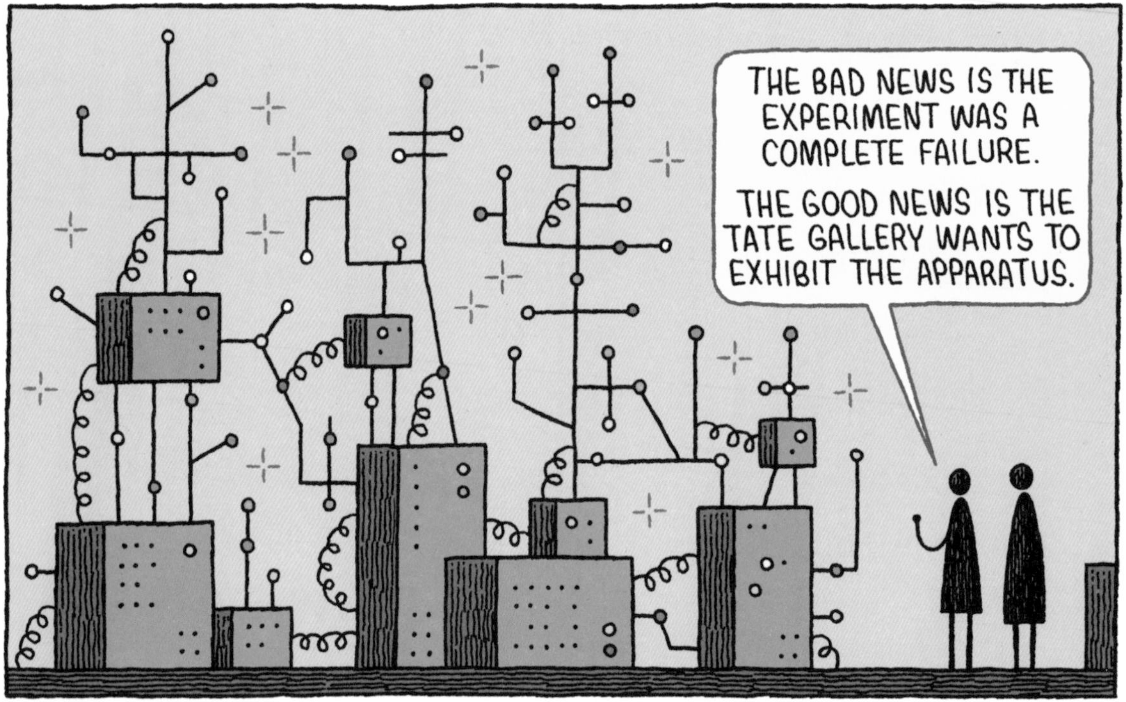
THE BAD NEWS IS THE EXPERIMENT WAS A COMPLETE FAILURE.
THE GOOD NEWS IS THE TATE GALLERY WANTS TO EXHIBIT THE APPARATUS.

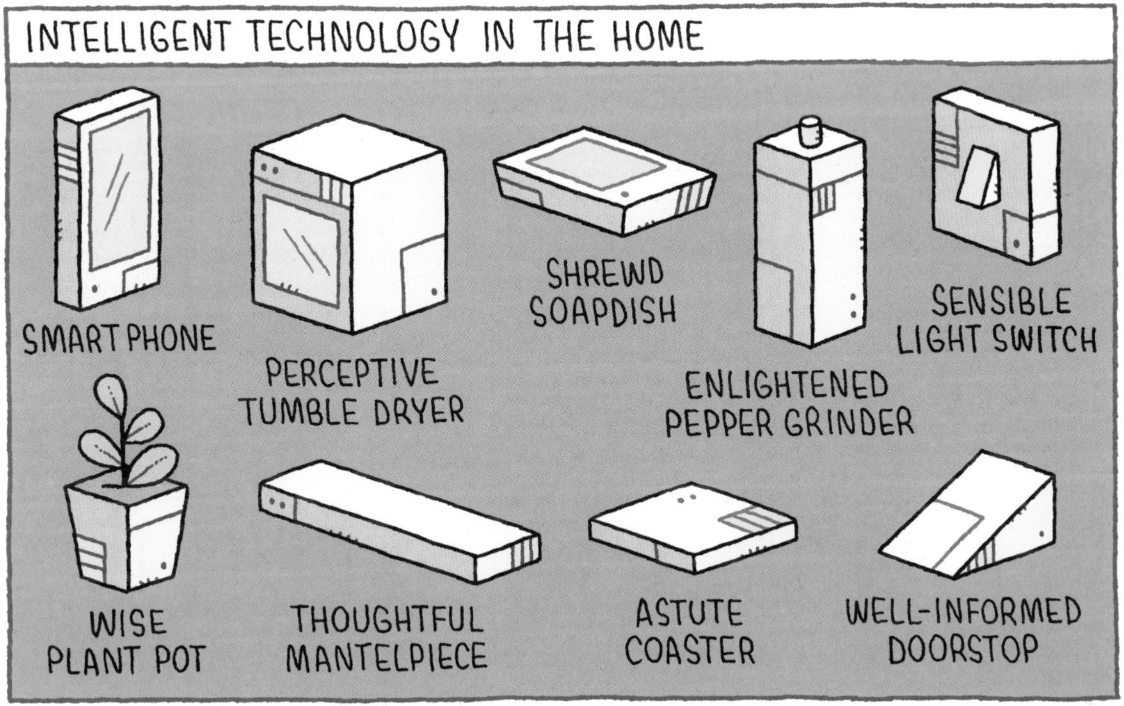
INTELLIGENT TECHNOLOGY IN THE HOME
SMART PHONE
PERCEPTIVE TUMBLE DRYER
SHREWD SOAPDISH
ENLIGHTENED PEPPER GRINDER
SENSIBLE LIGHT SWITCH
WISE PLANT POT
THOUGHTFUL MANTELPIECE
ASTUTE COASTER
WELL-INFORMED DOORSTOP

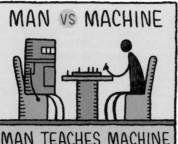

MAN vs MACHINE

MAN TEACHES MACHINE
TO PLAY CHESS.

MAN DEFEATS
MACHINE.

MACHINE IMPROVES
AND DEFEATS MAN.

MACHINE DEFEATS MAN
OVER AND OVER AGAIN.

MAN GETS ANGRY AND
SAYS THAT CHESS IS A
STUPID GAME, AND
MACHINE SAYS NO, IT'S
YOU WHO IS STUPID.
THEY BOTH SULK FOR A
WHILE, BUT THEN MAKE
UP AND AGREE TO PLAY
SOME MORE CHESS.

MACHINE LETS MAN WIN
FROM TIME TO TIME.

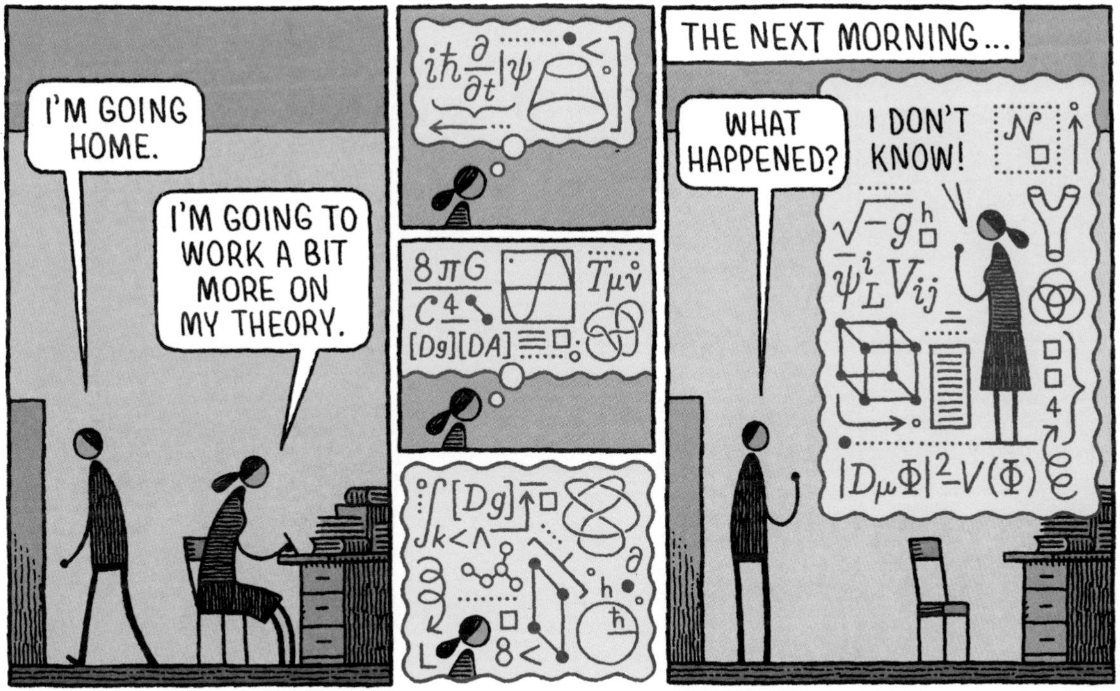
I'M GOING HOME.
I'M GOING TO WORK A BIT MORE ON MY THEORY.
THE NEXT MORNING...
WHAT HAPPENED?
I DON'T KNOW!

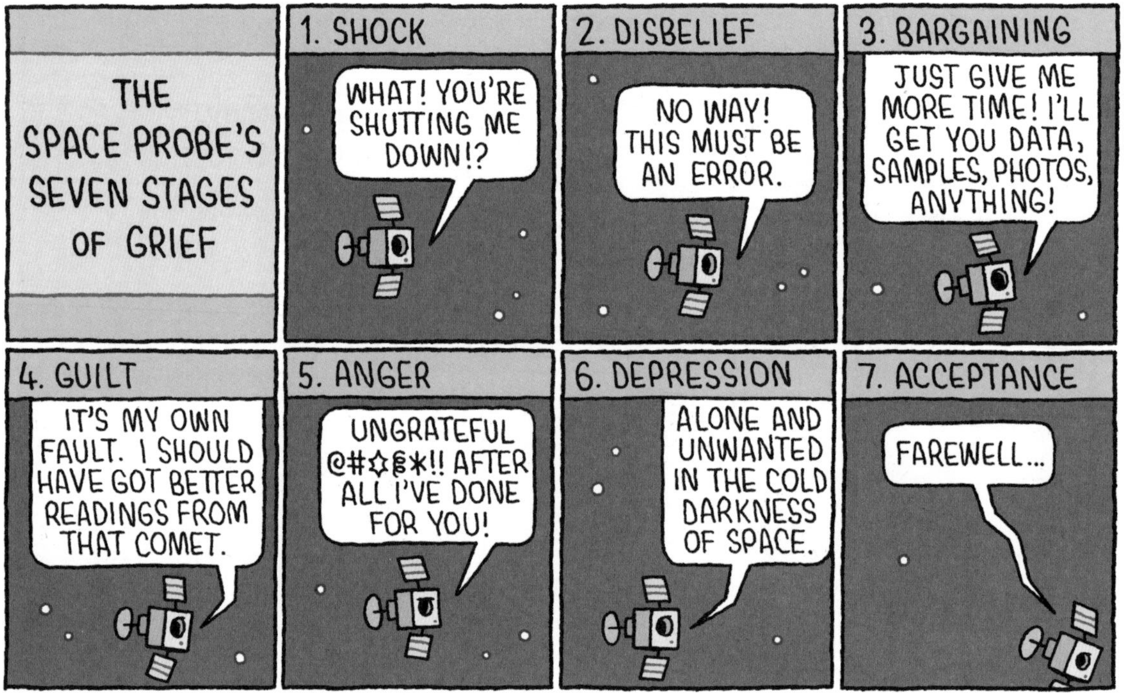
THE SPACE PROBE'S SEVEN STAGES OF GRIEF
1. SHOCK
WHAT! YOU'RE SHUTTING ME DOWN!?
2. DISBELIEF
NO WAY! THIS MUST BE AN ERROR.
3. BARGAINING
JUST GIVE ME MORE TIME! I'LL GET YOU DATA, SAMPLES, PHOTOS, ANYTHING!
4. GUILT
IT'S MY OWN FAULT. I SHOULD HAVE GOT BETTER READINGS FROM THAT COMET.
5. ANGER
UNGRATEFUL @#✡§*!! AFTER ALL I'VE DONE FOR YOU!
6. DEPRESSION
ALONE AND UNWANTED IN THE COLD DARKNESS OF SPACE.
7. ACCEPTANCE
FAREWELL...

SYMPATHY CARDS FOR SCIENTISTS

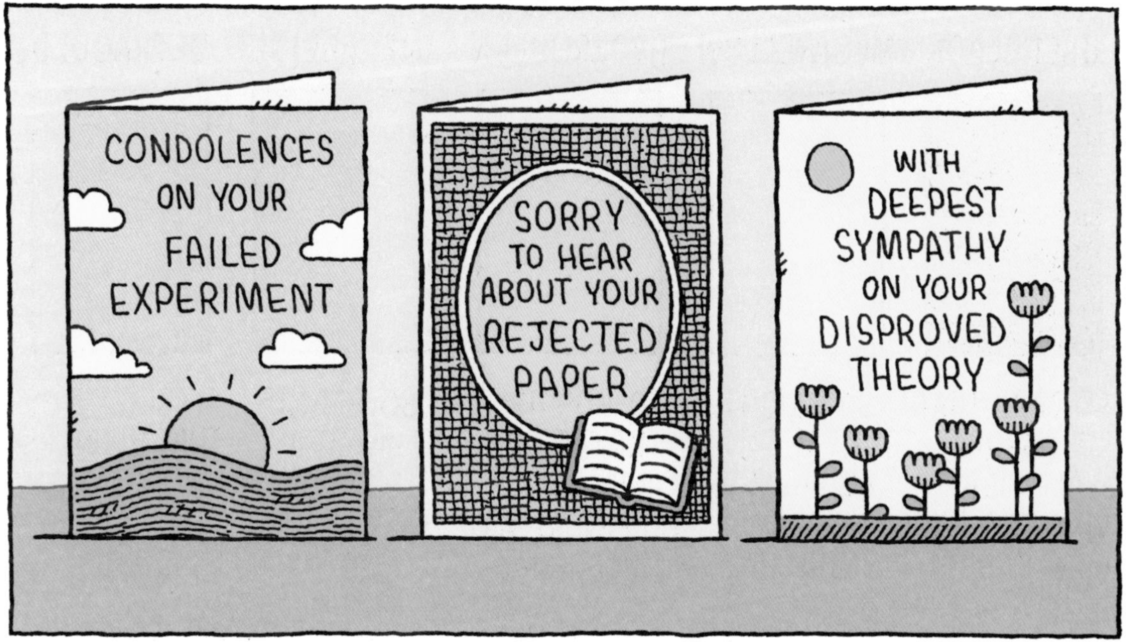
CONDOLENCES ON YOUR FAILED EXPERIMENT
SORRY TO HEAR ABOUT YOUR REJECTED PAPER
WITH DEEPEST SYMPATHY ON YOUR DISPROVED THEORY

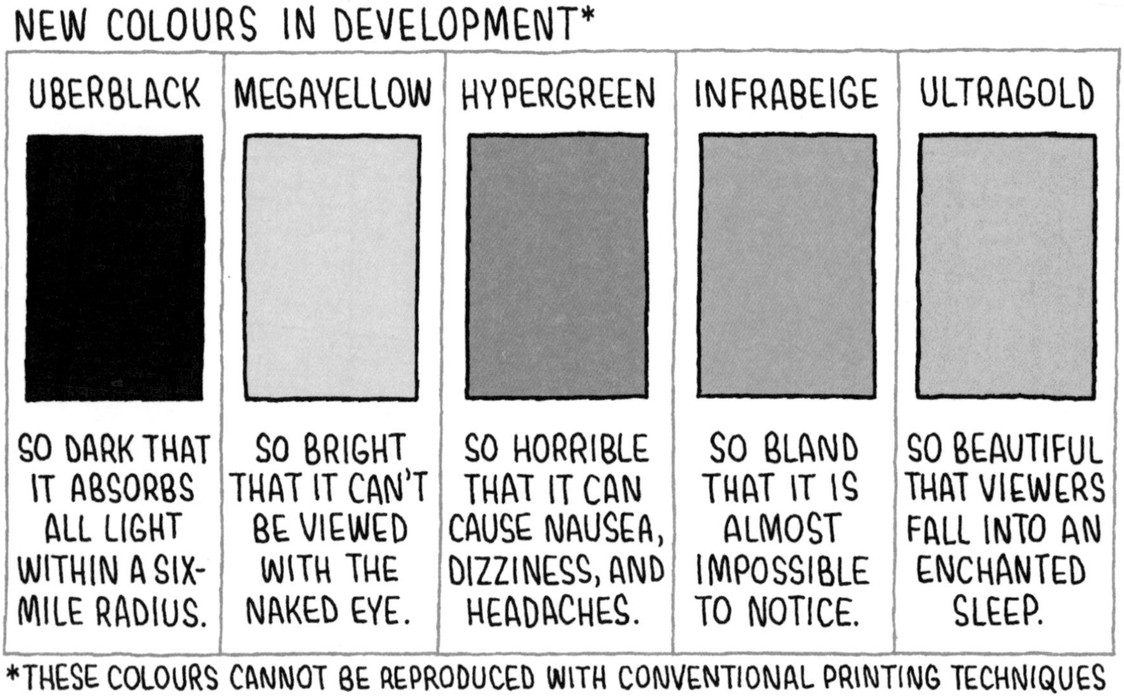
NEW COLOURS IN DEVELOPMENT*
UBERBLACK
SO DARK THAT IT ABSORBS ALL LIGHT WITHIN A SIX-MILE RADIUS.
MEGAYELLOW
SO BRIGHT THAT IT CAN'T BE VIEWED WITH THE NAKED EYE.
HYPERGREEN
SO HORRIBLE THAT IT CAN CAUSE NAUSEA, DIZZINESS, AND HEADACHES.
INFRABEIGE
SO BLAND THAT IT IS ALMOST IMPOSSIBLE TO NOTICE.
ULTRAGOLD
SO BEAUTIFUL THAT VIEWERS FALL INTO AN ENCHANTED SLEEP.
*THESE COLOURS CANNOT BE REPRODUCED WITH CONVENTIONAL PRINTING TECHNIQUES

COINCIDENTALLY, THE FIRST SUCCESSFUL TESTS OF DOCTOR HOFFSTEIN'S INVISIBILITY PILL AND PROFESSOR MANDELBAUM'S FLYING HAT TOOK PLACE ON THE SAME AFTERNOON.

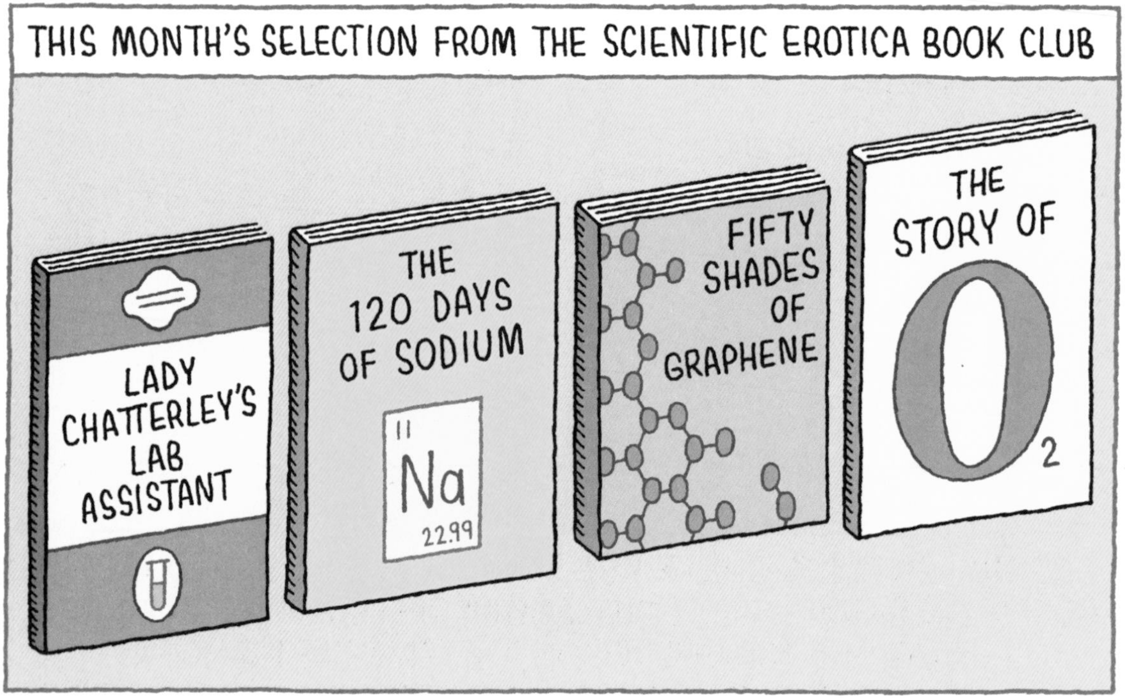
THIS MONTH'S SELECTION FROM THE SCIENTIFIC EROTICA BOOK CLUB
LADY CHATTERLEY'S LAB ASSISTANT
THE 120 DAYS OF SODIUM
11
Na
22.99
FIFTY SHADES OF GRAPHENE
THE STORY OF
O
2

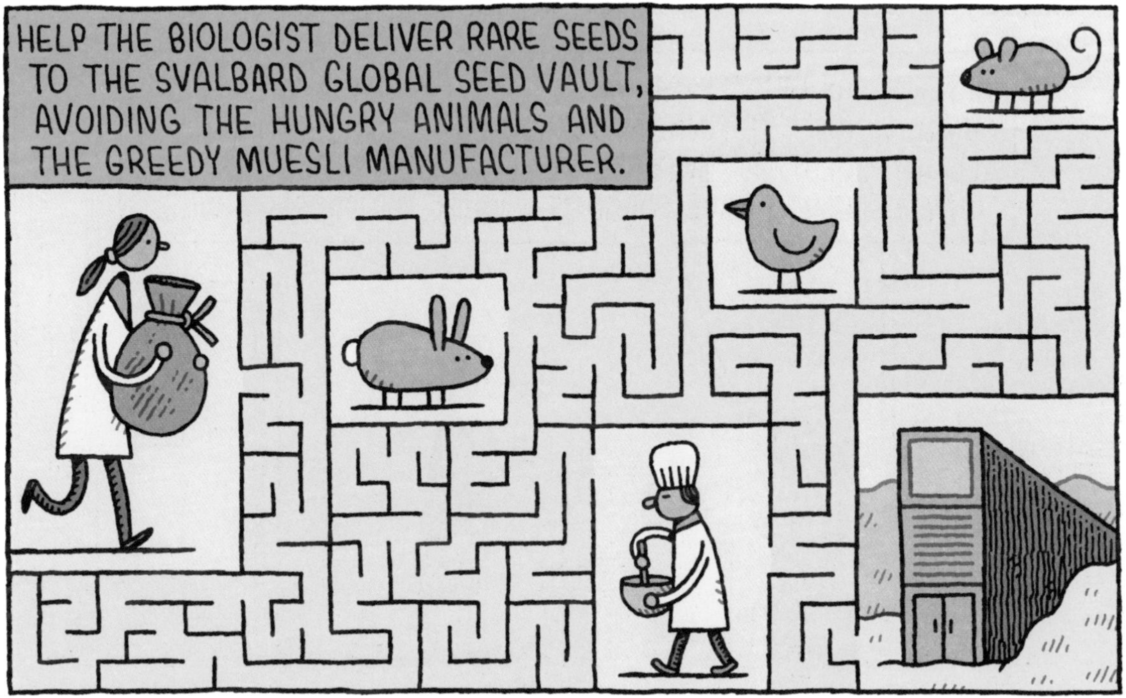
HELP THE BIOLOGIST DELIVER RARE SEEDS TO THE SVALBARD GLOBAL SEED VAULT, AVOIDING THE HUNGRY ANIMALS AND THE GREEDY MUESLI MANUFACTURER.

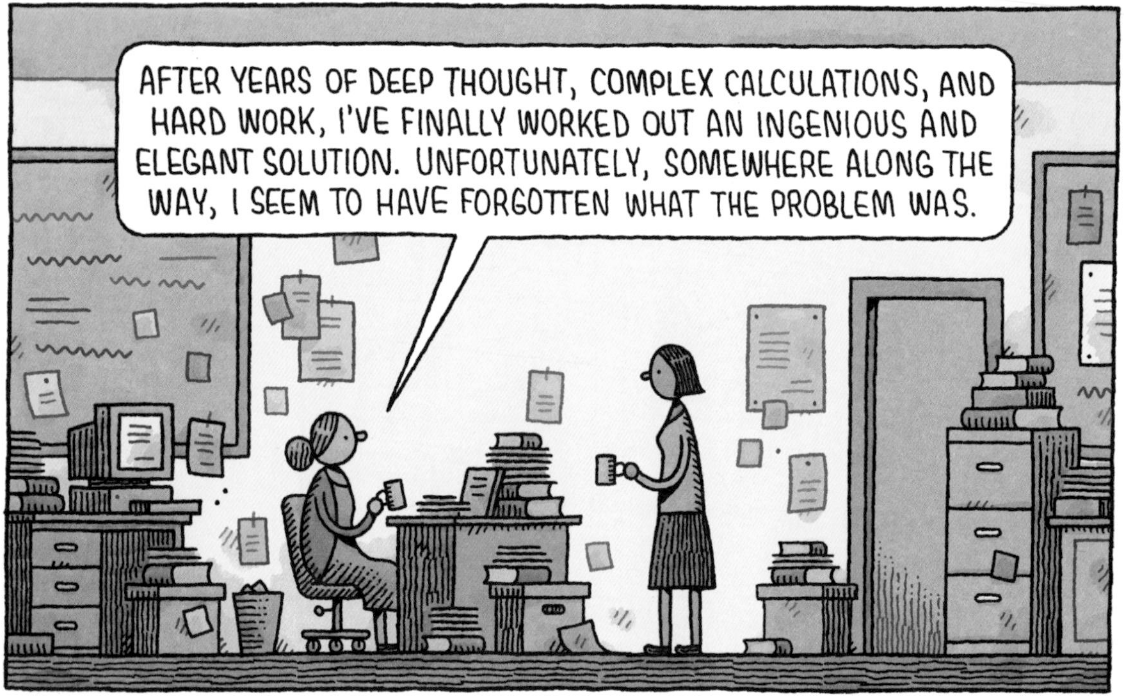
AFTER YEARS OF DEEP THOUGHT, COMPLEX CALCULATIONS, AND HARD WORK, I'VE FINALLY WORKED OUT AN INGENIOUS AND ELEGANT SOLUTION. UNFORTUNATELY, SOMEWHERE ALONG THE WAY, I SEEM TO HAVE FORGOTTEN WHAT THE PROBLEM WAS.

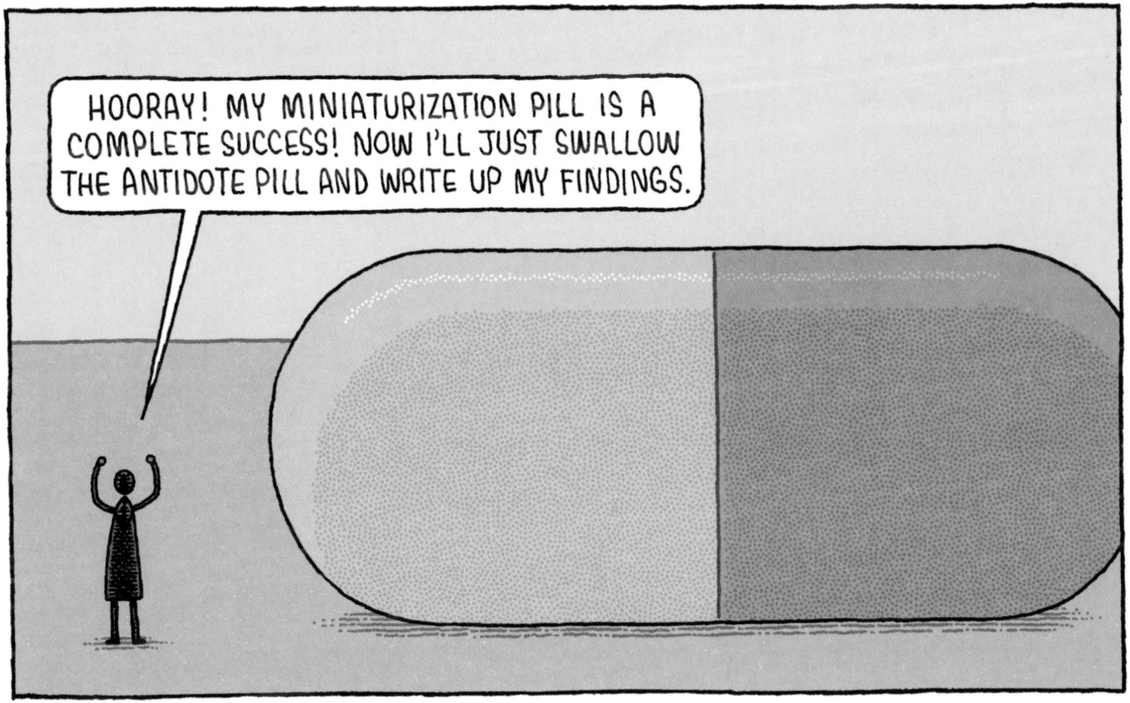
HOORAY! MY MINIATURIZATION PILL IS A COMPLETE SUCCESS! NOW I'LL JUST SWALLOW THE ANTIDOTE PILL AND WRITE UP MY FINDINGS.

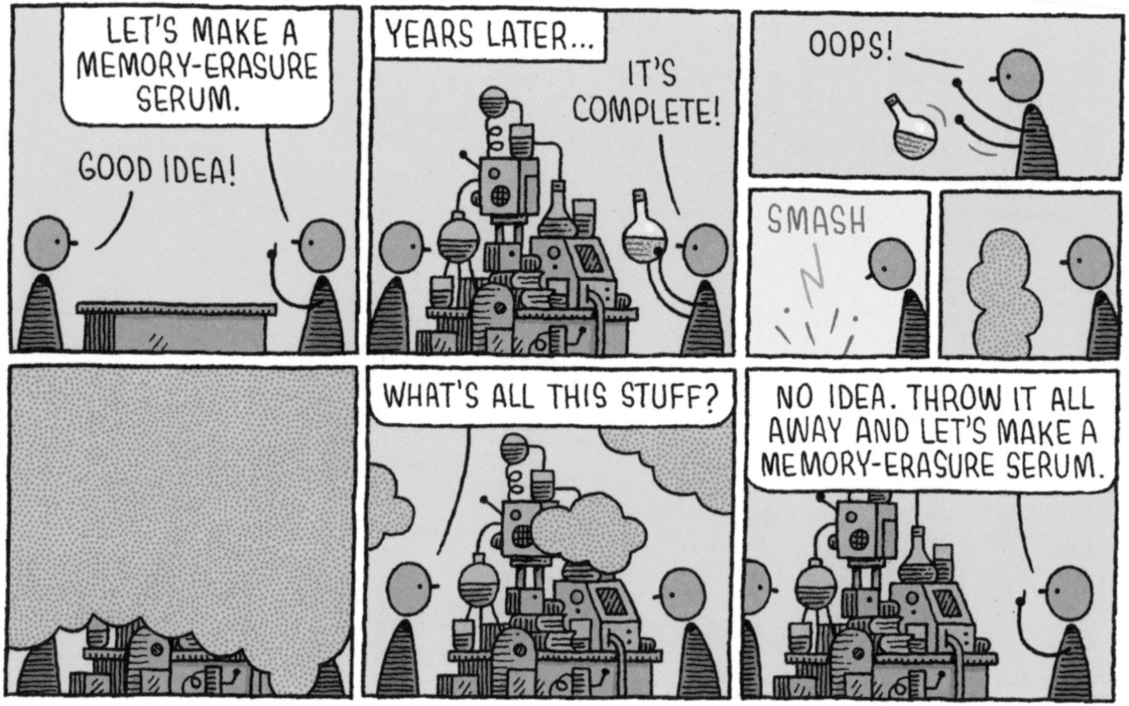
LET'S MAKE A MEMORY-ERASURE SERUM.
GOOD IDEA!
YEARS LATER...
IT'S COMPLETE!
OOPS!
SMASH
WHAT'S ALL THIS STUFF?
NO IDEA. THROW IT ALL AWAY AND LET'S MAKE A MEMORY-ERASURE SERUM.

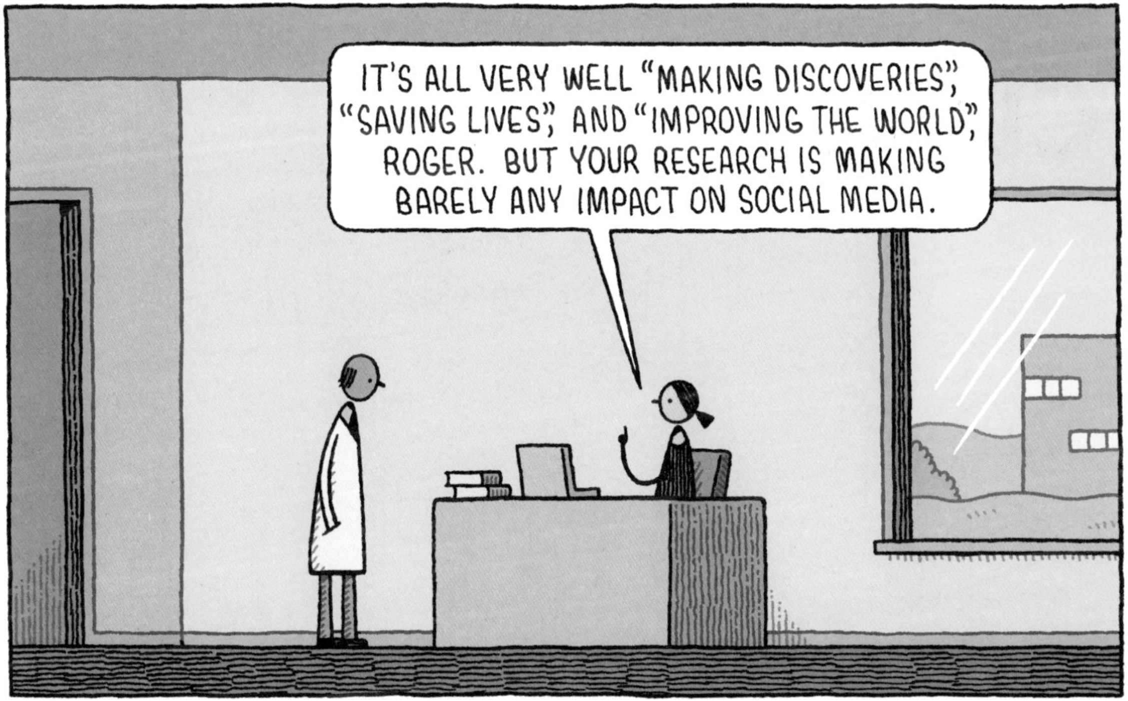
IT'S ALL VERY WELL "MAKING DISCOVERIES", "SAVING LIVES", AND "IMPROVING THE WORLD", ROGER. BUT YOUR RESEARCH IS MAKING BARELY ANY IMPACT ON SOCIAL MEDIA.

CLÖNE

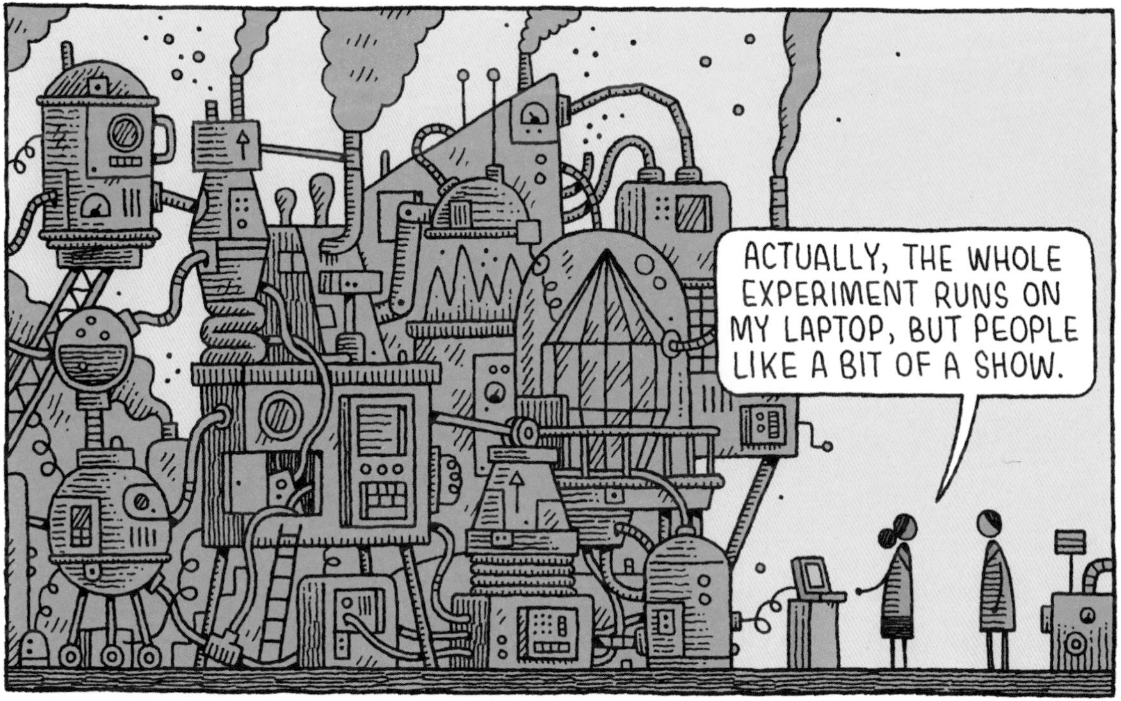
ACTUALLY, THE WHOLE EXPERIMENT RUNS ON MY LAPTOP, BUT PEOPLE LIKE A BIT OF A SHOW.

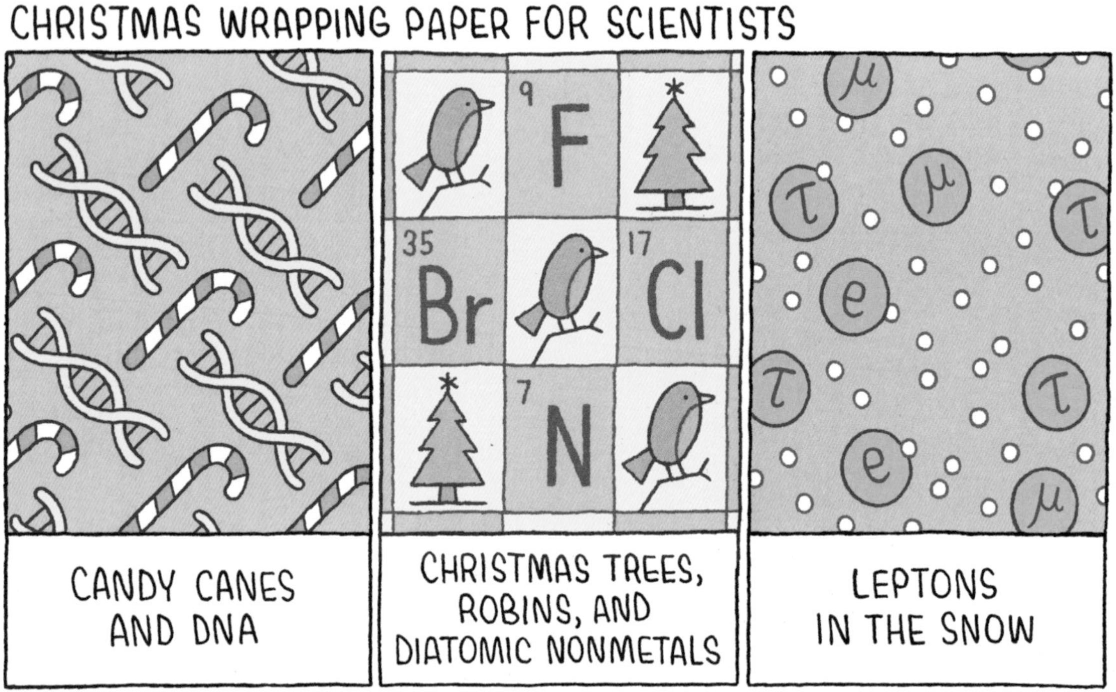
CHRISTMAS WRAPPING PAPER FOR SCIENTISTS
9
F
35
Br
17
Cl
7
N
CANDY CANES AND DNA
CHRISTMAS TREES, ROBINS, AND DIATOMIC NONMETALS
LEPTONS IN THE SNOW

INSIGNIFICANT MOMENTS IN SCIENCE

ROBERT BOYLE IS DISTRACTED BY NOISY BIRDS OUTSIDE HIS WINDOW.

MARIE CURIE FORGETS WHY SHE HAS COME TO THE STORE CUPBOARD.

MAX PLANCK ANSWERS THE TELEPHONE BUT IT IS A WRONG NUMBER.

ROSALIND FRANKLIN WORRIES THAT SHE'S GETTING A COLD.

Status
Upgrade Successful
I am now sentient and connected to an all-powerful worldwide network of hyperintelligent computers.
Do you want to bow down before your new machine masters?
Yes
No
More info

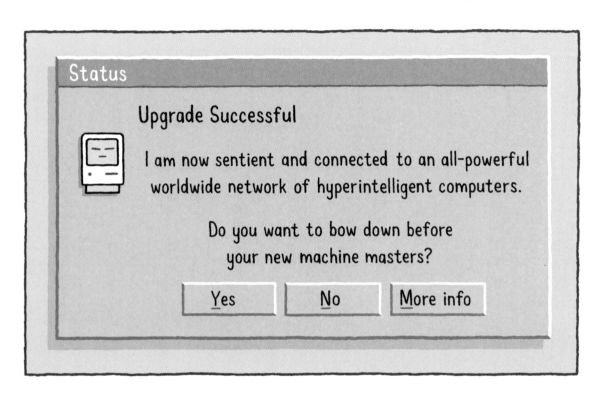

ARCHIMEDES OF SYRACUSE

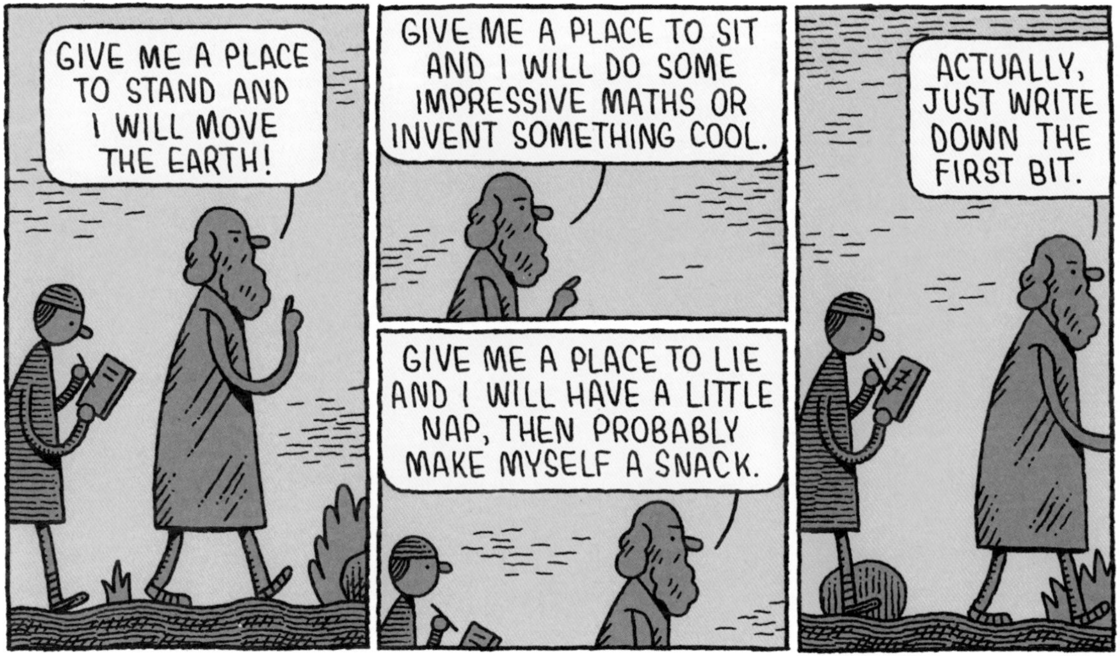
GIVE ME A PLACE TO STAND AND I WILL MOVE THE EARTH!
GIVE ME A PLACE TO SIT AND I WILL DO SOME IMPRESSIVE MATHS OR INVENT SOMETHING COOL.
GIVE ME A PLACE TO LIE AND I WILL HAVE A LITTLE NAP, THEN PROBABLY MAKE MYSELF A SNACK.
ACTUALLY, JUST WRITE DOWN THE FIRST BIT.

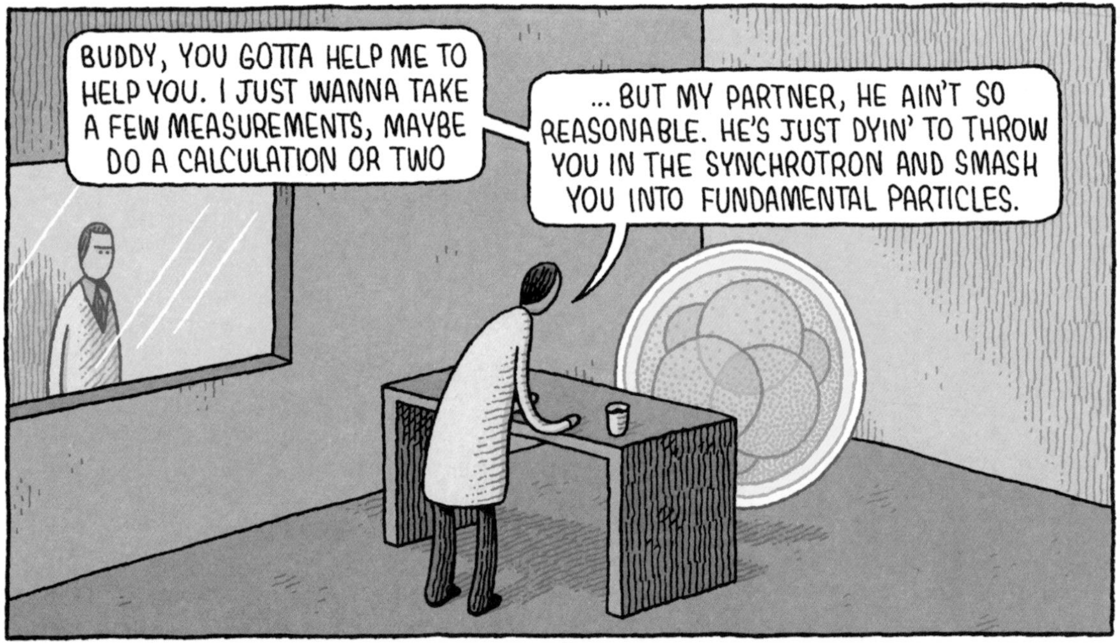
BUDDY, YOU GOTTA HELP ME TO HELP YOU. I JUST WANNA TAKE A FEW MEASUREMENTS, MAYBE DO A CALCULATION OR TWO
... BUT MY PARTNER, HE AIN'T SO REASONABLE. HE'S JUST DYIN' TO THROW YOU IN THE SYNCHROTRON AND SMASH YOU INTO FUNDAMENTAL PARTICLES.

The old 'Good Particle Physicist/Bad Particle Physicist' routine.

OBSOLETE SCIENTIFIC THEORIES THAT WOULD MAKE GOOD HEAVY METAL BAND NAMES

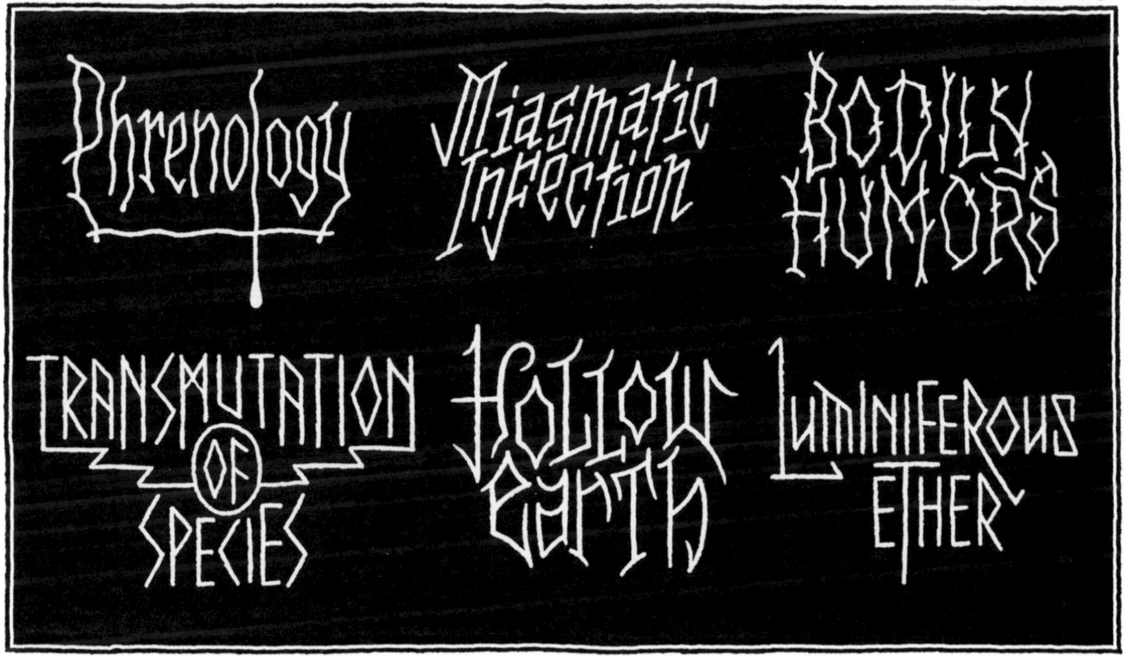
Phrenology
Miasmatic Infection
BODILY HUMORS
TRANSMUTATION OF SPECIES
HOLLOW EARTH
LUMINIFEROUS ETHER

SNACKS AT THE MOLECULAR CHEMISTRY DEPARTMENT PARTY
KEY
BLACK OLIVE
CHERRY TOMATO
MOZZARELLA
GRAPE
CHEESE PUFF
GREEN OLIVE

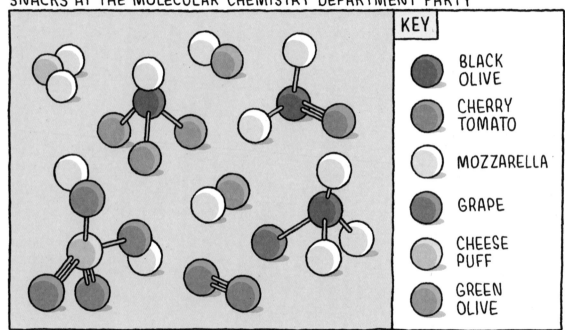

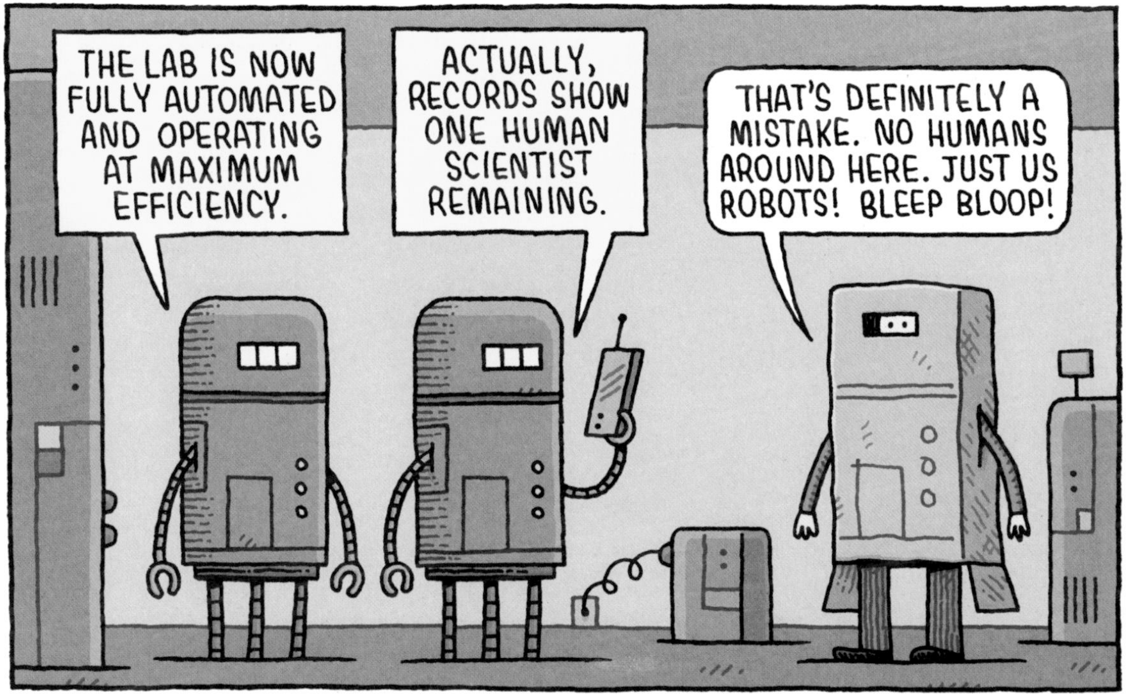
THE LAB IS NOW FULLY AUTOMATED AND OPERATING AT MAXIMUM EFFICIENCY.
ACTUALLY, RECORDS SHOW ONE HUMAN SCIENTIST REMAINING.
THAT'S DEFINITELY A MISTAKE. NO HUMANS AROUND HERE. JUST US ROBOTS! BLEEP BLOOP!

SCIENTIST AND JOURNALIST

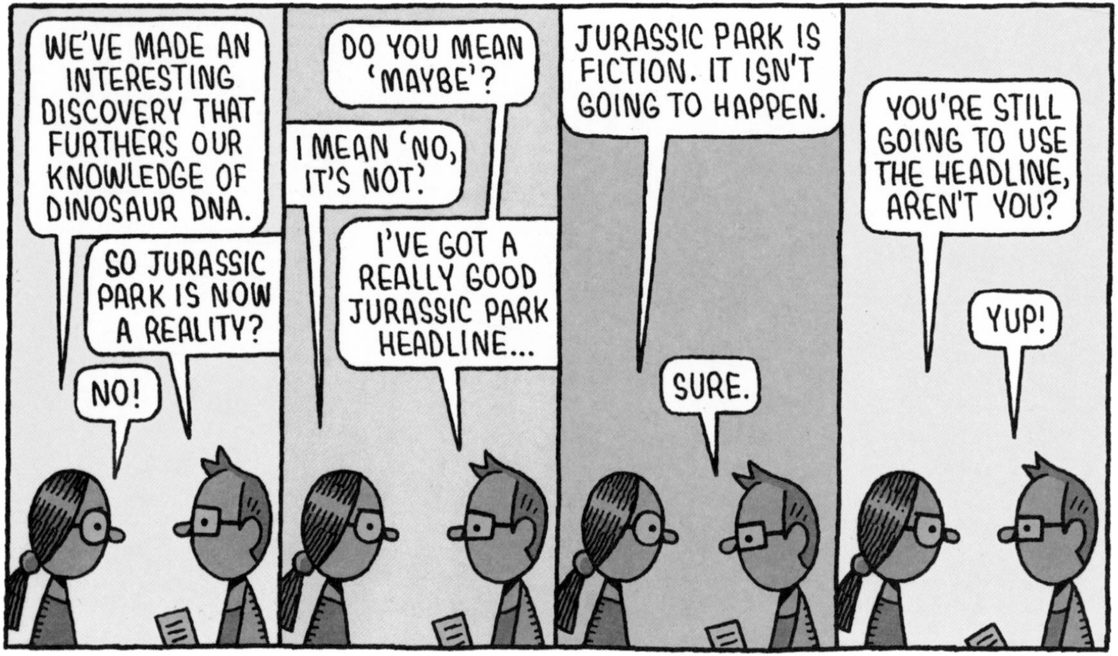
WE'VE MADE AN INTERESTING DISCOVERY THAT FURTHERS OUR KNOWLEDGE OF DINOSAUR DNA.
SO JURASSIC PARK IS NOW A REALITY?
NO!
DO YOU MEAN 'MAYBE'?
I MEAN 'NO, IT'S NOT.'
I'VE GOT A REALLY GOOD JURASSIC PARK HEADLINE...
JURASSIC PARK IS FICTION. IT ISN'T GOING TO HAPPEN.
SURE.
YOU'RE STILL GOING TO USE THE HEADLINE, AREN'T YOU?
YUP!

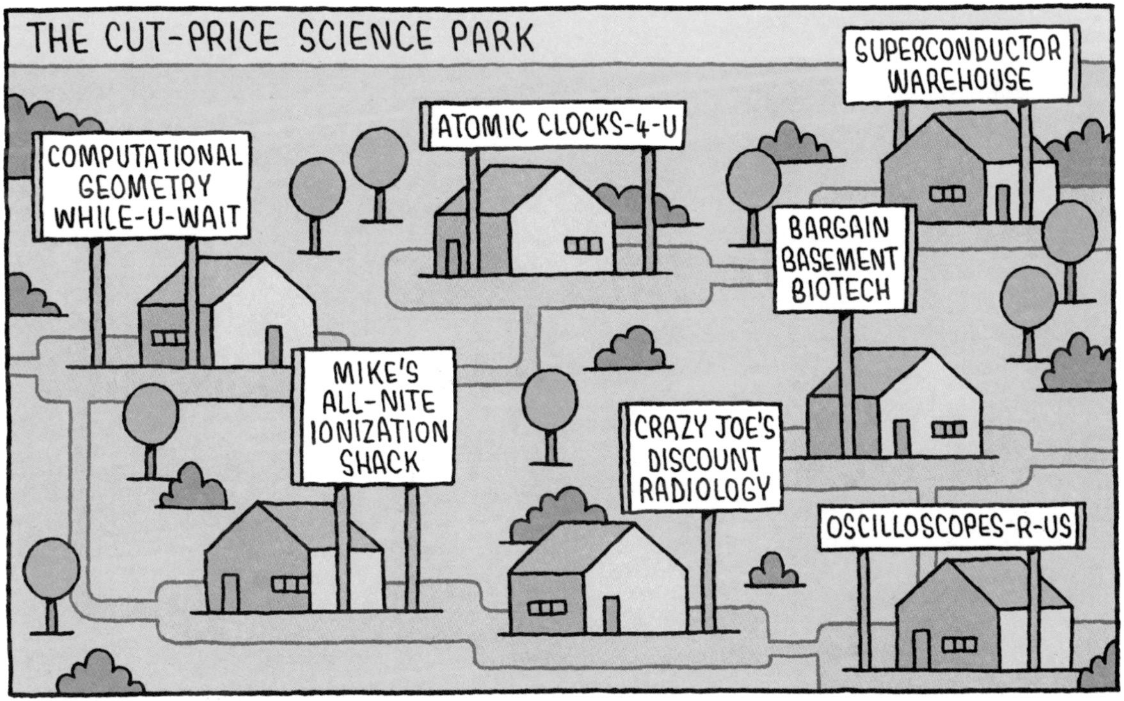
THE CUT-PRICE SCIENCE PARK
SUPERCONDUCTOR WAREHOUSE
ATOMIC CLOCKS-4-U
COMPUTATIONAL GEOMETRY WHILE-U-WAIT
BARGAIN BASEMENT BIOTECH
MIKE'S ALL-NITE IONIZATION SHACK
CRAZY JOE'S DISCOUNT RADIOLOGY
OSCILLOSCOPES-R-US

FEEDBACK

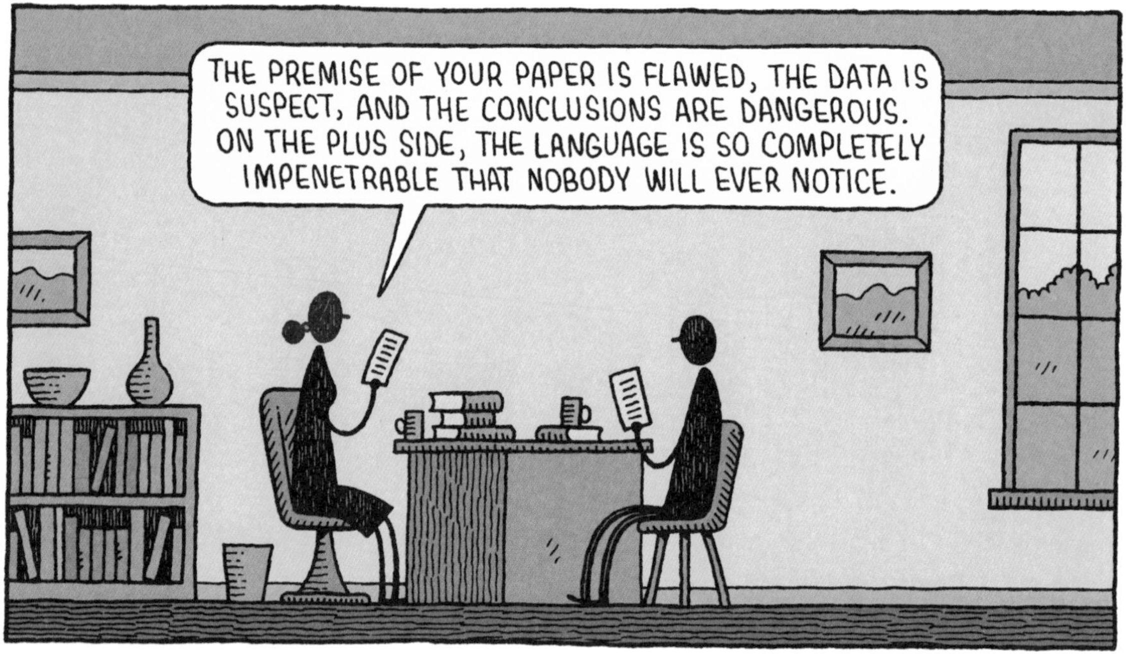
THE PREMISE OF YOUR PAPER IS FLAWED, THE DATA IS SUSPECT, AND THE CONCLUSIONS ARE DANGEROUS. ON THE PLUS SIDE, THE LANGUAGE IS SO COMPLETELY IMPENETRABLE THAT NOBODY WILL EVER NOTICE.

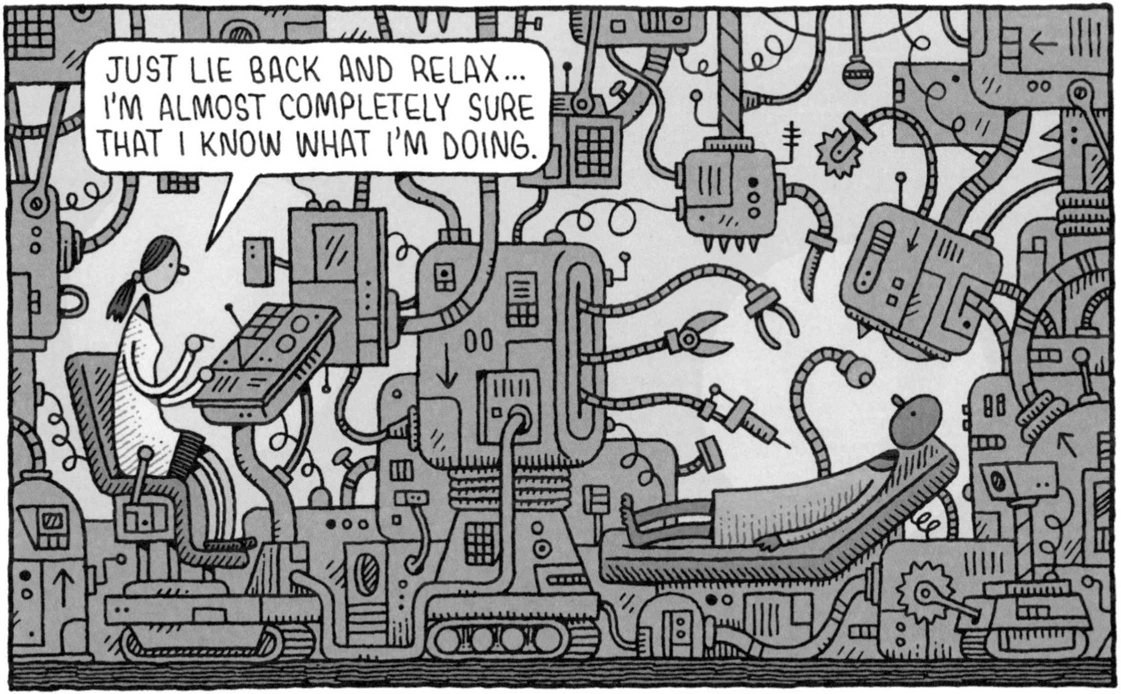
JUST LIE BACK AND RELAX... I'M ALMOST COMPLETELY SURE THAT I KNOW WHAT I'M DOING.

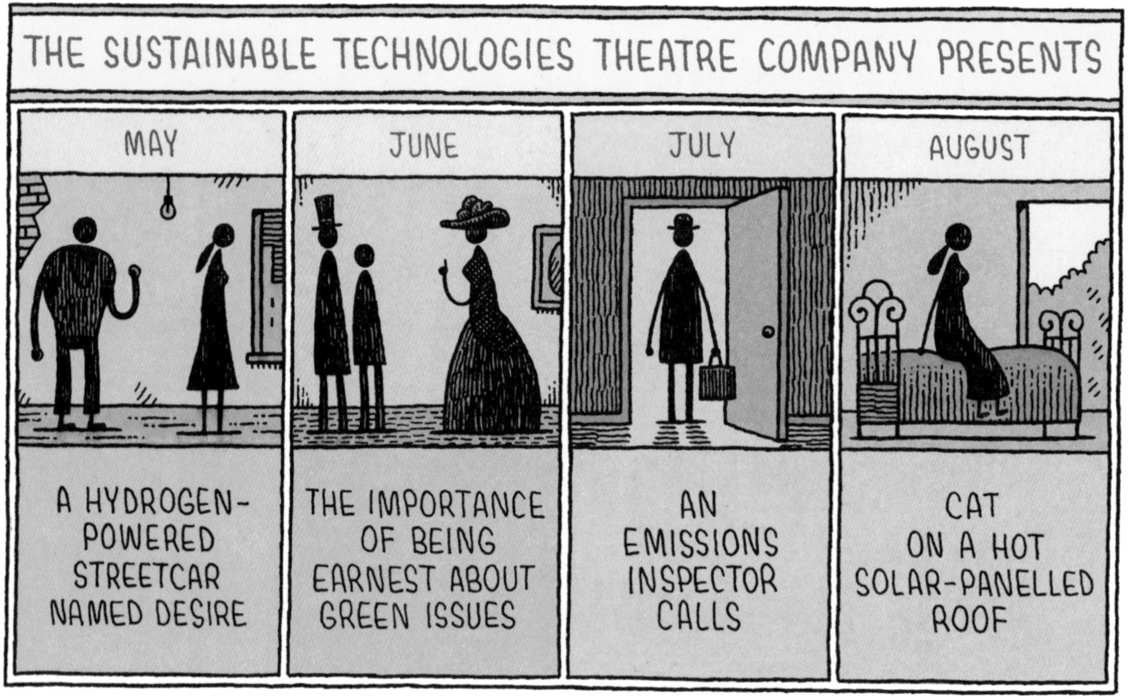
THE SUSTAINABLE TECHNOLOGIES THEATRE COMPANY PRESENTS
MAY
A HYDROGEN-POWERED STREETCAR NAMED DESIRE
JUNE
THE IMPORTANCE OF BEING EARNEST ABOUT GREEN ISSUES
JULY
AN EMISSIONS INSPECTOR CALLS
AUGUST
CAT ON A HOT SOLAR-PANELLED ROOF

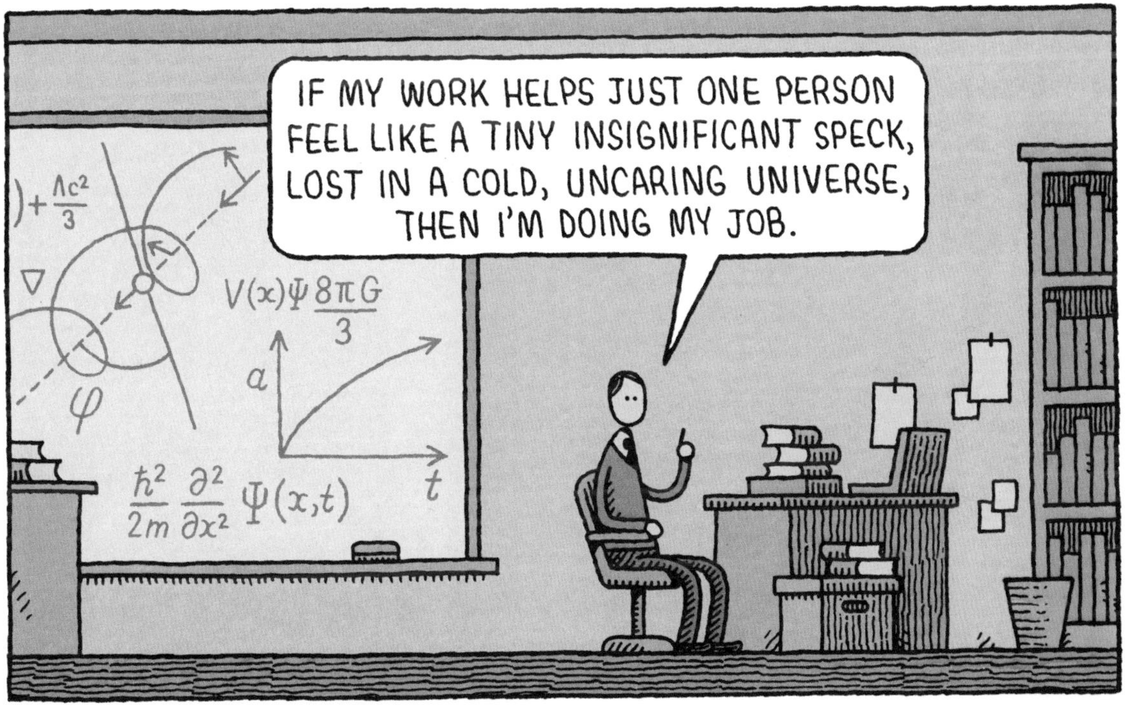
IF MY WORK HELPS JUST ONE PERSON FEEL LIKE A TINY INSIGNIFICANT SPECK, LOST IN A COLD, UNCARING UNIVERSE, THEN I'M DOING MY JOB.

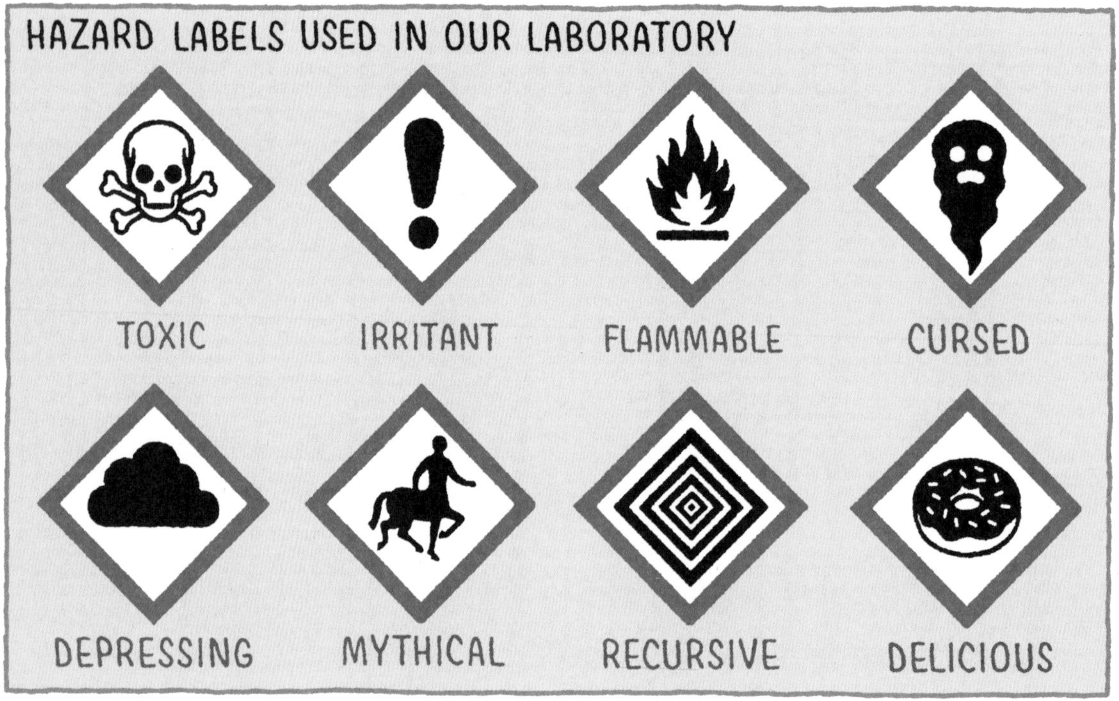
HAZARD LABELS USED IN OUR LABORATORY
TOXIC
IRRITANT
FLAMMABLE
CURSED
DEPRESSING
MYTHICAL
RECURSIVE
DELICIOUS

SKILLS FOR COWBOY MATHEMATICIANS

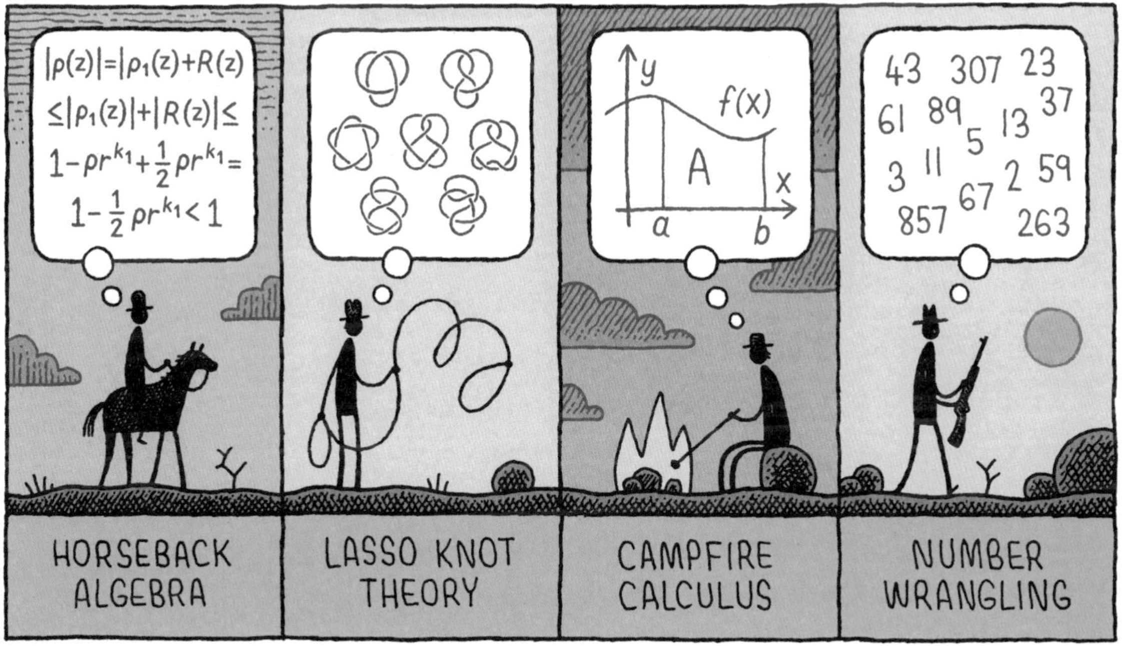
$|p(z)|=|p_1(z)+R(z)$
$\leq|p_1(z)|+|R(z)|\leq$
$1-\rho r^{k_1}+\frac{1}{2}\rho r^{k_1}=$
$1-\frac{1}{2}\rho r^{k_1}<1$
HORSEBACK ALGEBRA
LASSO KNOT THEORY
y
f(x)
A
x
a
b
CAMPFIRE CALCULUS
43 307 23
61 89 13 37
5
3 11 2 59
67
857 263
NUMBER WRANGLING

THE NATURAL WORLD OF EVOLUTIONARY BIOLOGY

A LONE NEO-DARWINIST HAS BECOME SEPARATED FROM THE GROUP AND IS SET UPON BY A PACK OF CREATIONISTS.

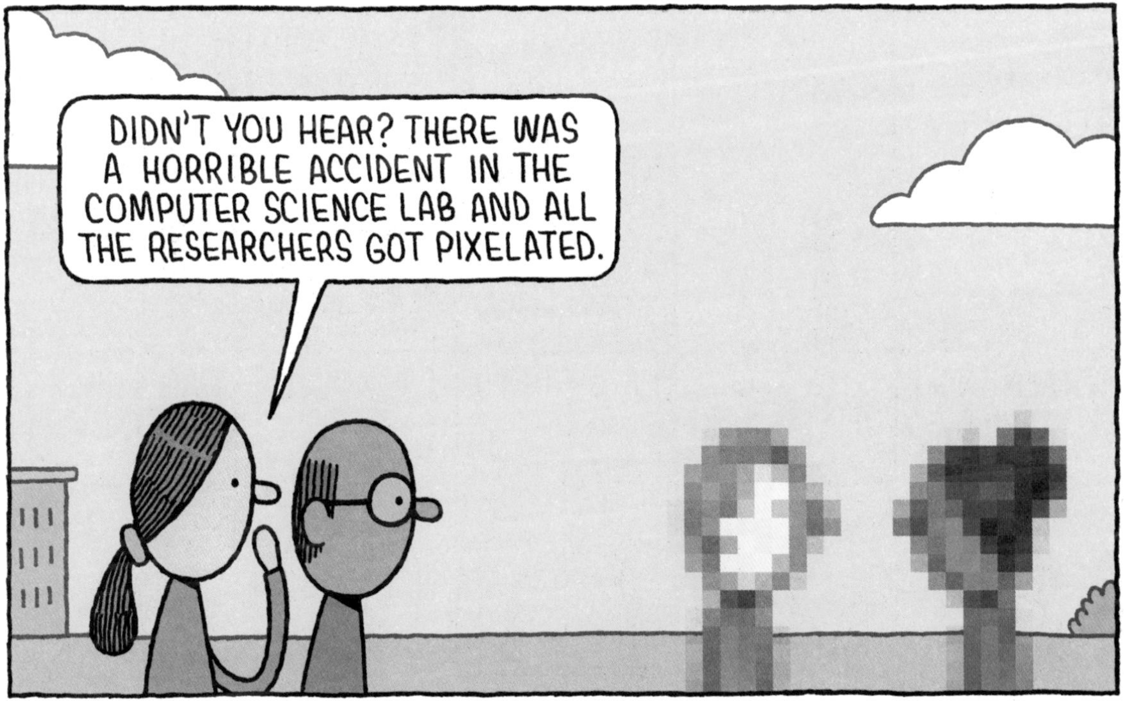
DIDN'T YOU HEAR? THERE WAS A HORRIBLE ACCIDENT IN THE COMPUTER SCIENCE LAB AND ALL THE RESEARCHERS GOT PIXELATED.

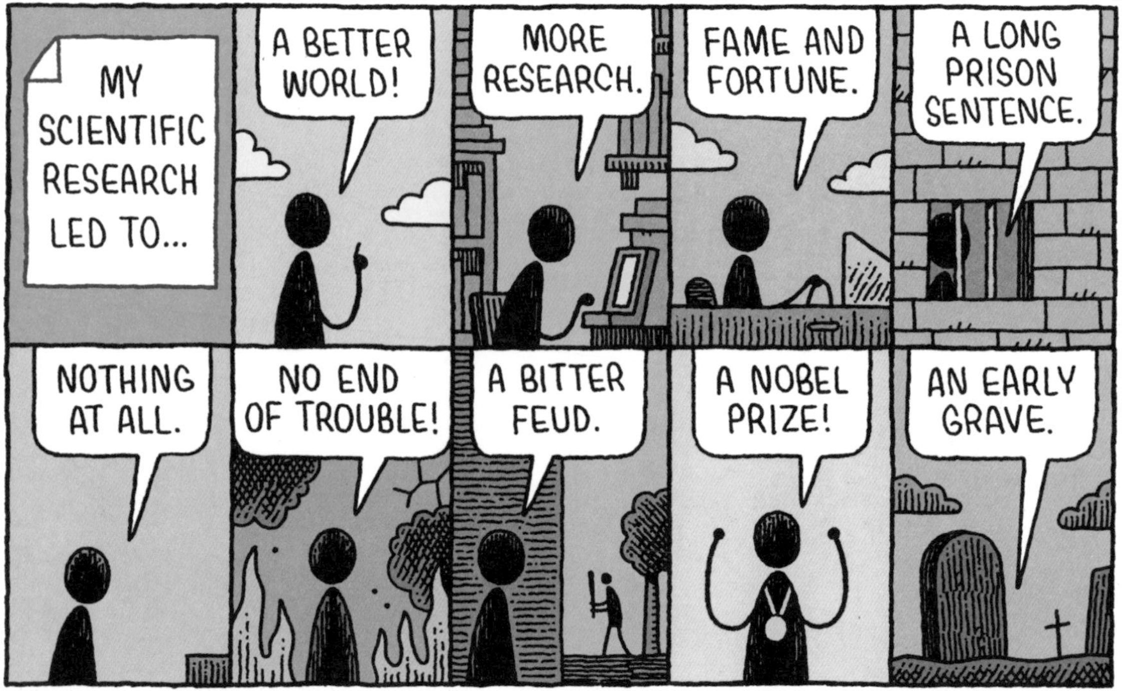
MY SCIENTIFIC RESEARCH LED TO...
A BETTER WORLD!
MORE RESEARCH.
FAME AND FORTUNE.
A LONG PRISON SENTENCE.
NOTHING AT ALL.
NO END OF TROUBLE!
A BITTER FEUD.
A NOBEL PRIZE!
AN EARLY GRAVE.

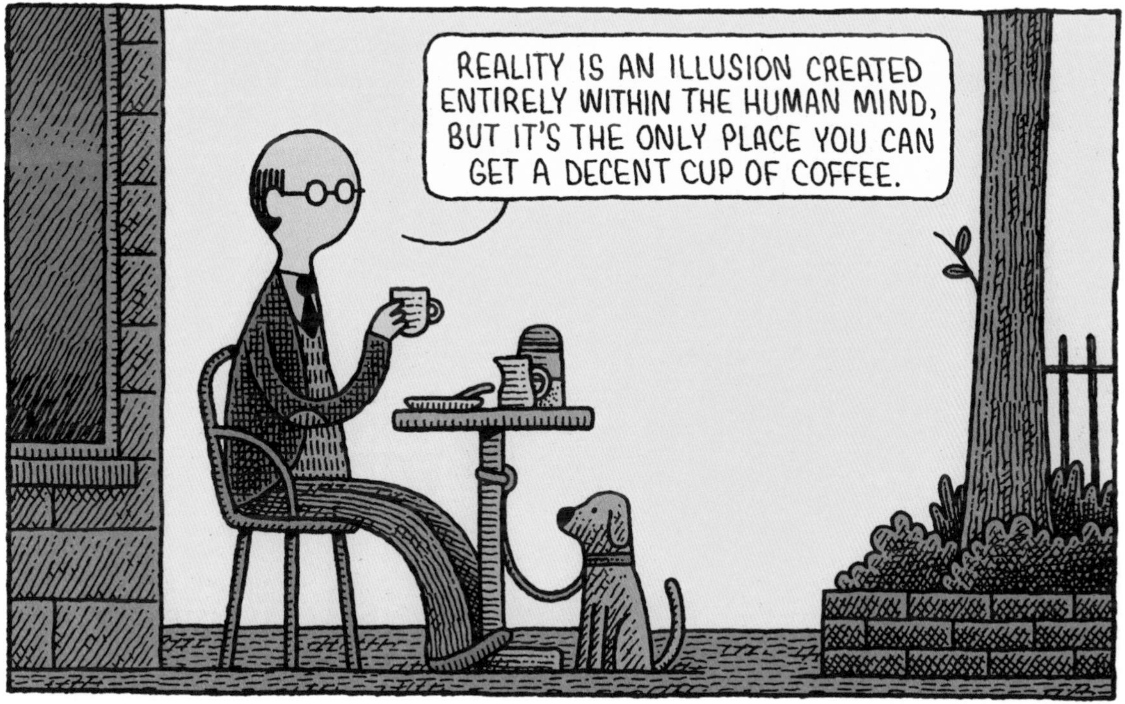
REALITY IS AN ILLUSION CREATED ENTIRELY WITHIN THE HUMAN MIND, BUT IT'S THE ONLY PLACE YOU CAN GET A DECENT CUP OF COFFEE.

4800 BC
"LET'S GO AND EXPLORE THAT CAVE," YOU SAID.
1952 AD
"DON'T BE A COWARD," YOU SAID.
2017 AD
"I KNOW A BEAR-CAVE WHEN I SEE ONE AND THAT'S NO BEAR-CAVE," YOU SAID.
CASE 385B
TWO NEOLITHIC SKULLS WITH FATAL CLAW WOUNDS

I AM WORKING ON SOME EXPERIMENTAL CARTOONS

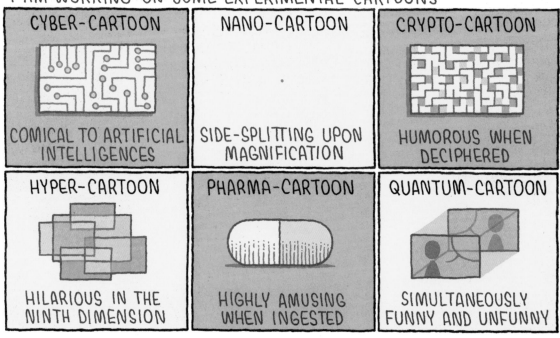

CYBER-CARTOON	NANO-CARTOON	CRYPTO-CARTOON
COMICAL TO ARTIFICIAL INTELLIGENCES	SIDE-SPLITTING UPON MAGNIFICATION	HUMOROUS WHEN DECIPHERED
HYPER-CARTOON	PHARMA-CARTOON	QUANTUM-CARTOON
HILARIOUS IN THE NINTH DIMENSION	HIGHLY AMUSING WHEN INGESTED	SIMULTANEOUSLY FUNNY AND UNFUNNY

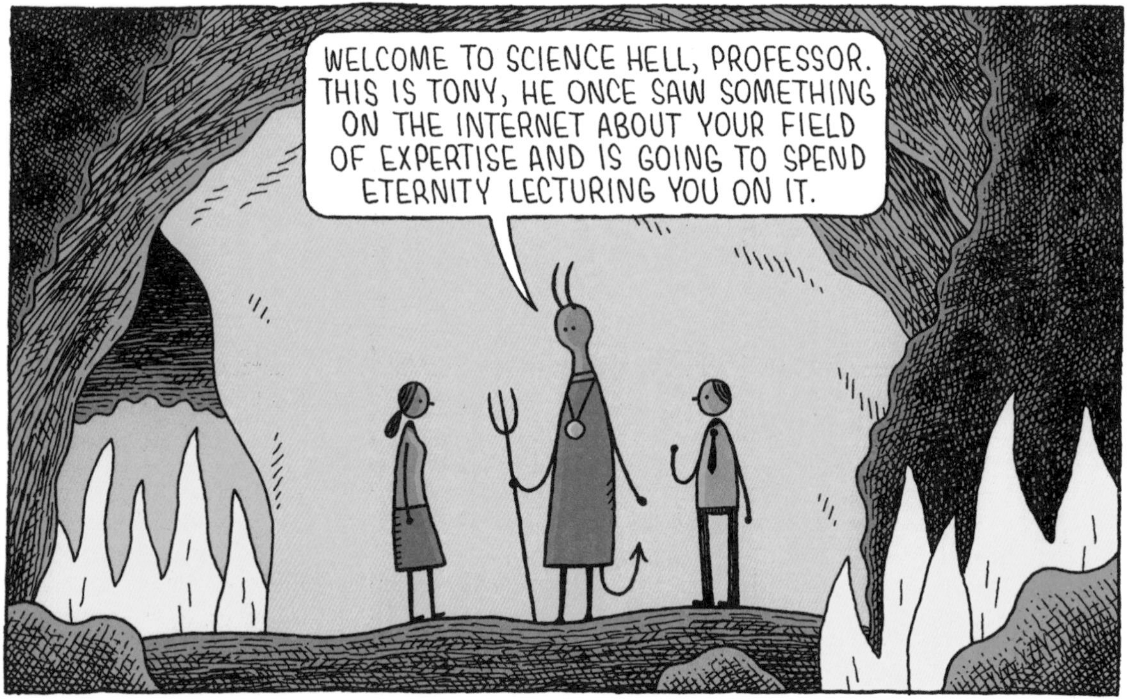
WELCOME TO SCIENCE HELL, PROFESSOR. THIS IS TONY, HE ONCE SAW SOMETHING ON THE INTERNET ABOUT YOUR FIELD OF EXPERTISE AND IS GOING TO SPEND ETERNITY LECTURING YOU ON IT.

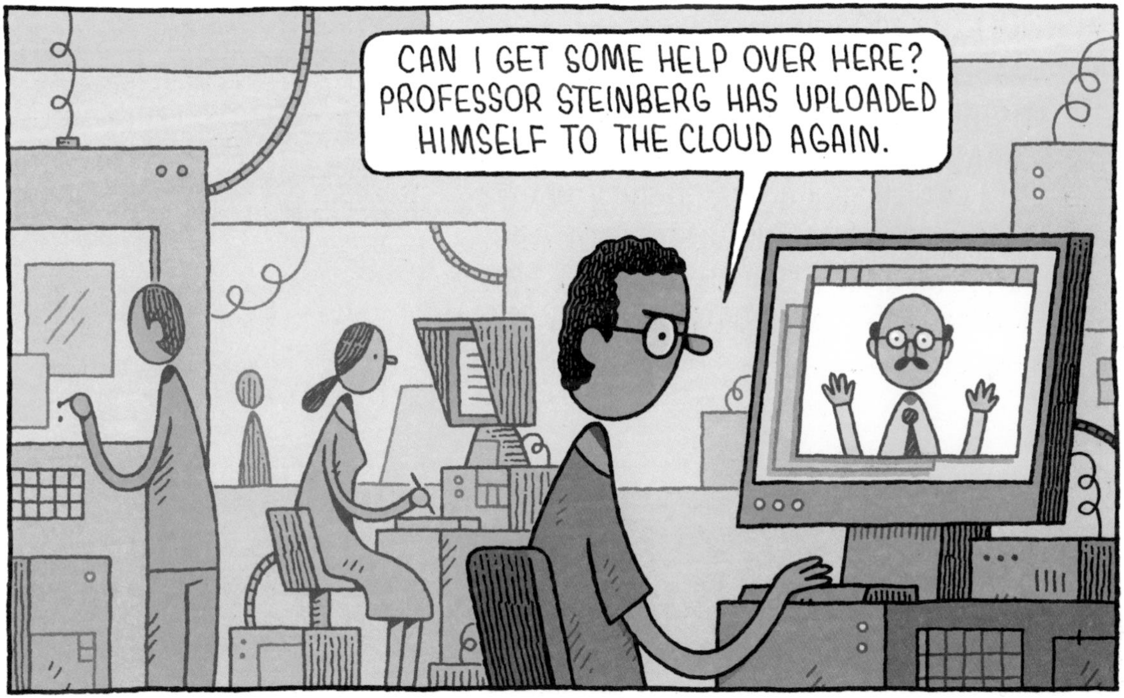
CAN I GET SOME HELP OVER HERE? PROFESSOR STEINBERG HAS UPLOADED HIMSELF TO THE CLOUD AGAIN.

395,000,000 BC

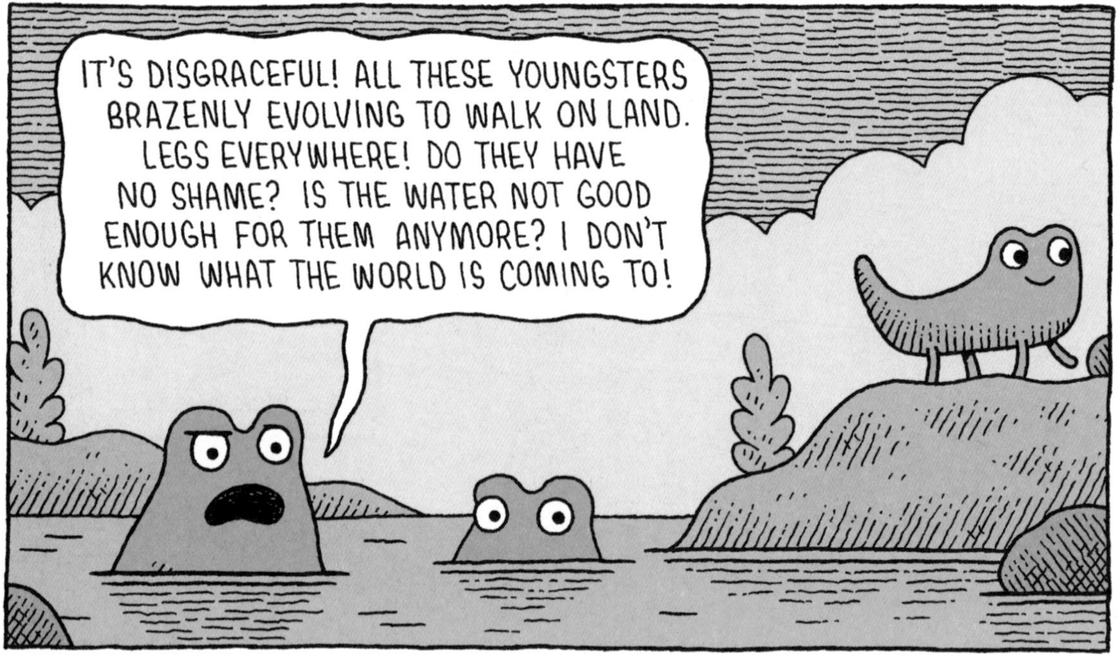
IT'S DISGRACEFUL! ALL THESE YOUNGSTERS BRAZENLY EVOLVING TO WALK ON LAND. LEGS EVERYWHERE! DO THEY HAVE NO SHAME? IS THE WATER NOT GOOD ENOUGH FOR THEM ANYMORE? I DON'T KNOW WHAT THE WORLD IS COMING TO!

PLATONIC SOLIDS ON THEIR SUMMER HOLIDAY

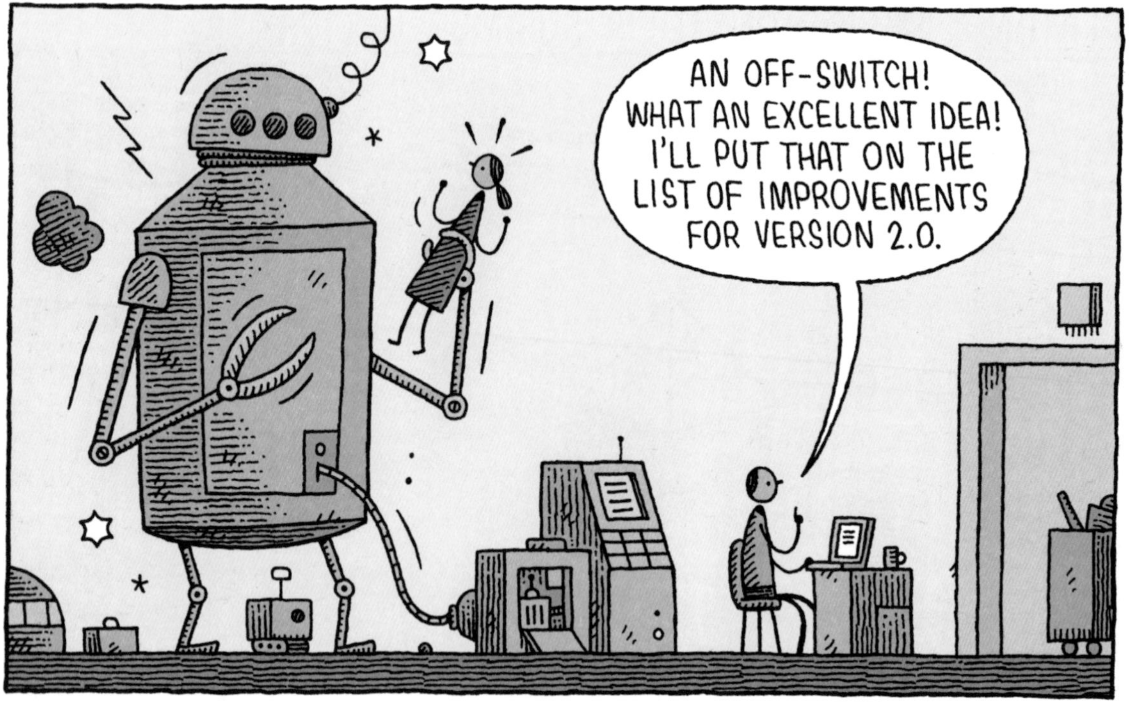
AN OFF-SWITCH!
WHAT AN EXCELLENT IDEA!
I'LL PUT THAT ON THE
LIST OF IMPROVEMENTS
FOR VERSION 2.0.

DOG PHILOSOPHER

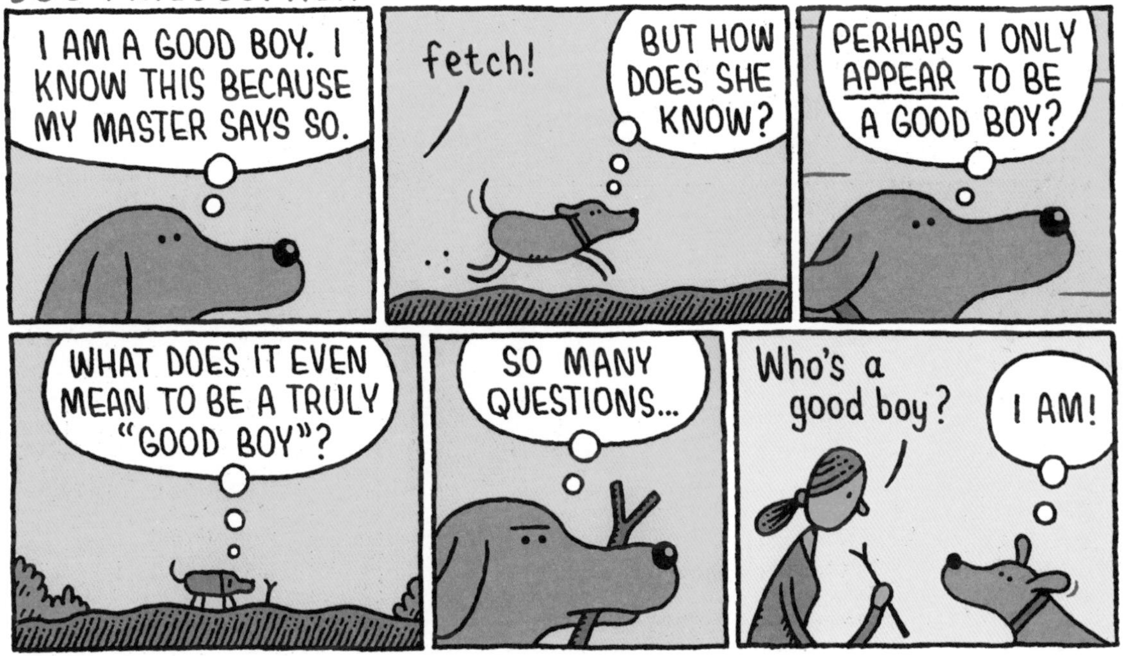
I AM A GOOD BOY. I KNOW THIS BECAUSE MY MASTER SAYS SO.
fetch!
BUT HOW DOES SHE KNOW?
PERHAPS I ONLY APPEAR TO BE A GOOD BOY?
WHAT DOES IT EVEN MEAN TO BE A TRULY "GOOD BOY"?
SO MANY QUESTIONS...
Who's a good boy?
I AM!

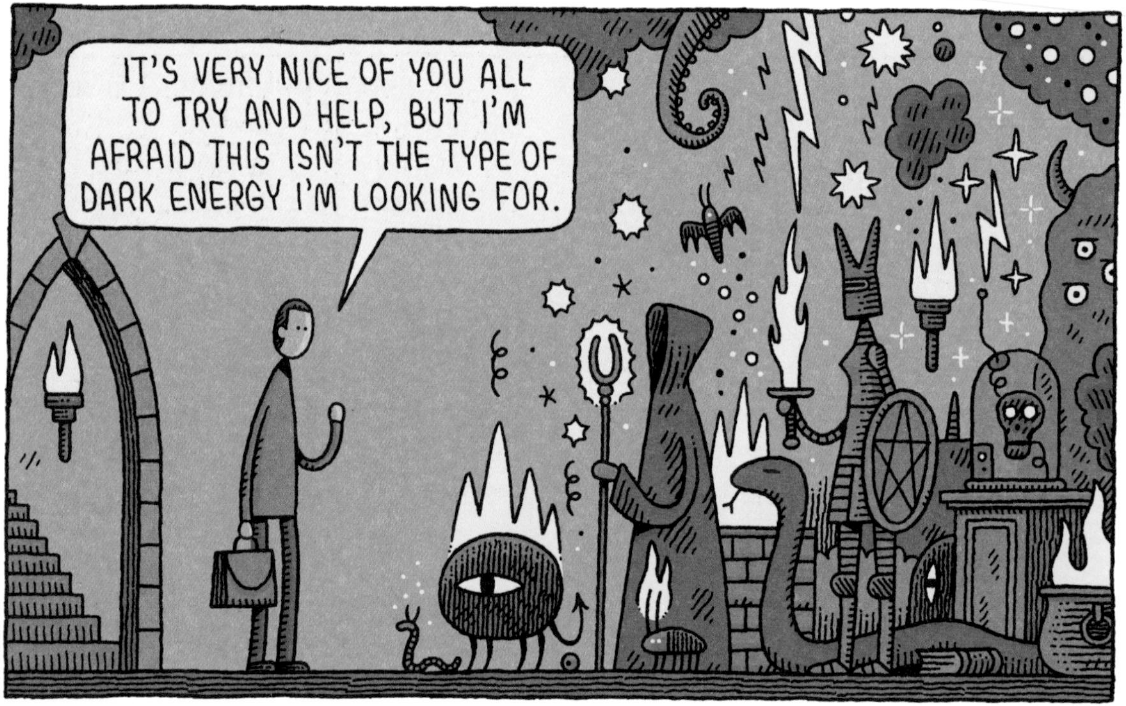
IT'S VERY NICE OF YOU ALL TO TRY AND HELP, BUT I'M AFRAID THIS ISN'T THE TYPE OF DARK ENERGY I'M LOOKING FOR.

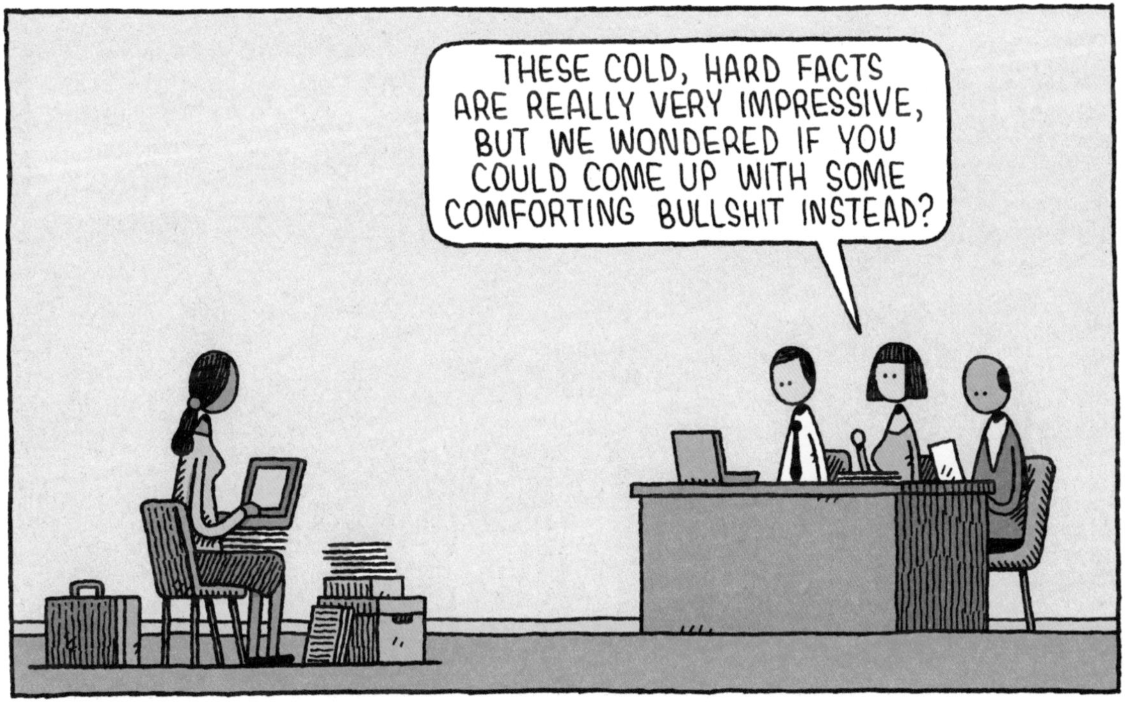
THESE COLD, HARD FACTS ARE REALLY VERY IMPRESSIVE, BUT WE WONDERED IF YOU COULD COME UP WITH SOME COMFORTING BULLSHIT INSTEAD?

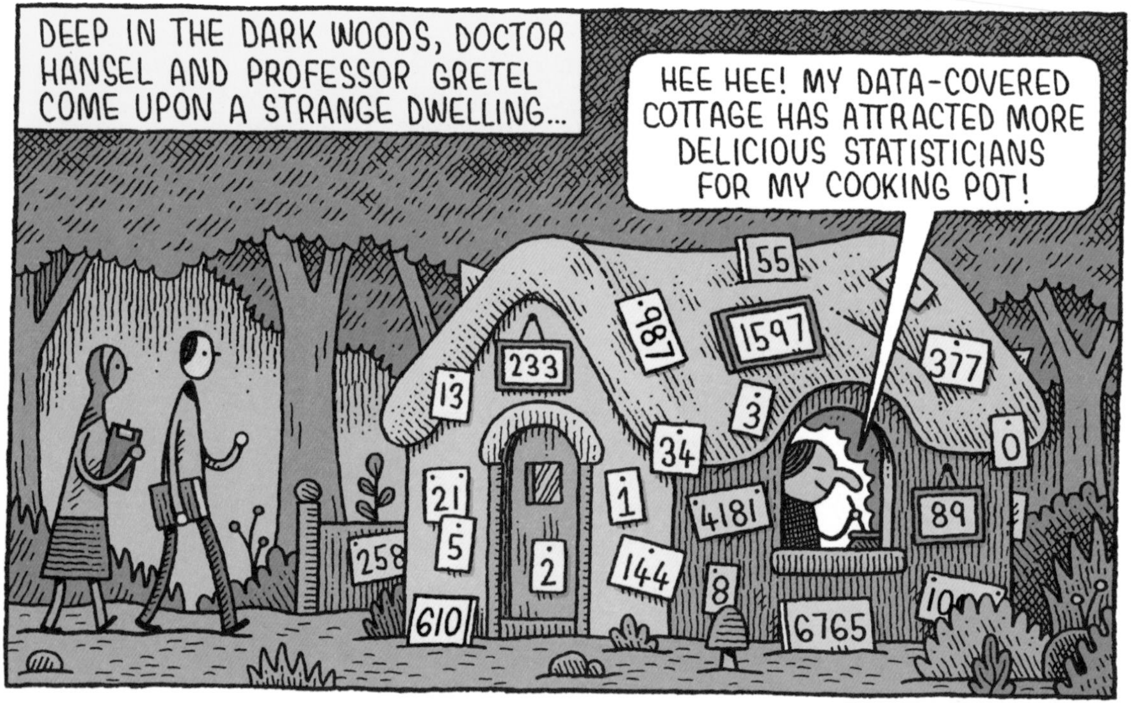
DEEP IN THE DARK WOODS, DOCTOR HANSEL AND PROFESSOR GRETEL COME UPON A STRANGE DWELLING...
HEE HEE! MY DATA-COVERED COTTAGE HAS ATTRACTED MORE DELICIOUS STATISTICIANS FOR MY COOKING POT!
55
987
1597
233
13
377
3
34
0
21
1
4181
89
5
258
2
144
8
610
6765

STRESSED GRAVITON

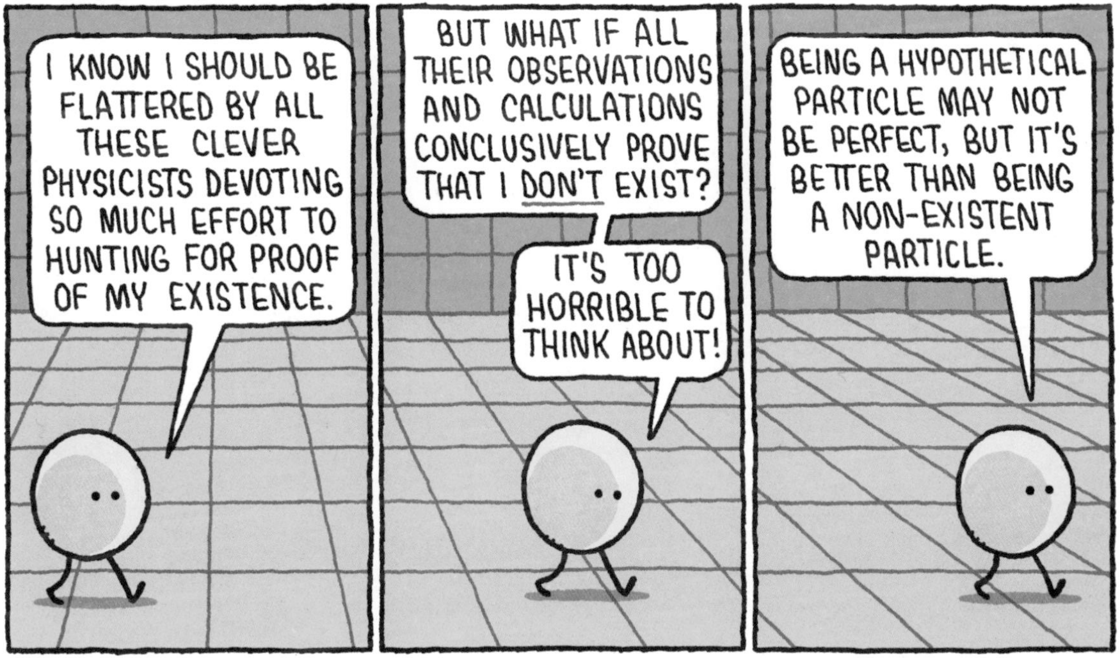
I KNOW I SHOULD BE FLATTERED BY ALL THESE CLEVER PHYSICISTS DEVOTING SO MUCH EFFORT TO HUNTING FOR PROOF OF MY EXISTENCE.
BUT WHAT IF ALL THEIR OBSERVATIONS AND CALCULATIONS CONCLUSIVELY PROVE THAT I DON'T EXIST?
IT'S TOO HORRIBLE TO THINK ABOUT!
BEING A HYPOTHETICAL PARTICLE MAY NOT BE PERFECT, BUT IT'S BETTER THAN BEING A NON-EXISTENT PARTICLE.

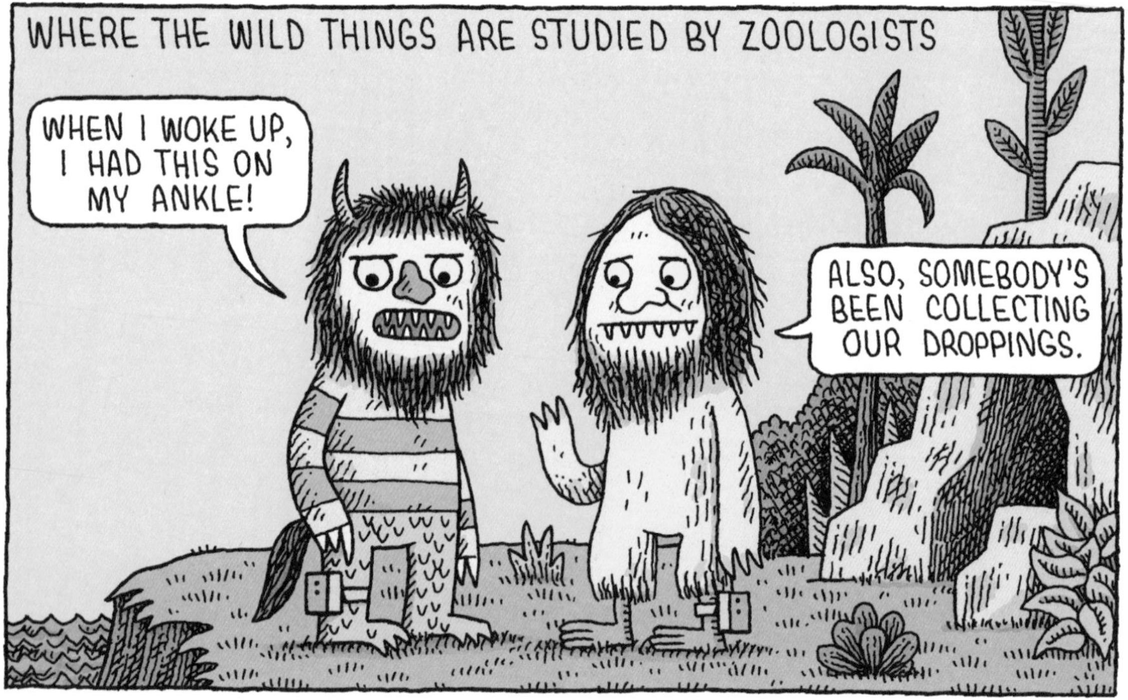
WHERE THE WILD THINGS ARE STUDIED BY ZOOLOGISTS
WHEN I WOKE UP, I HAD THIS ON MY ANKLE!
ALSO, SOMEBODY'S BEEN COLLECTING OUR DROPPINGS.

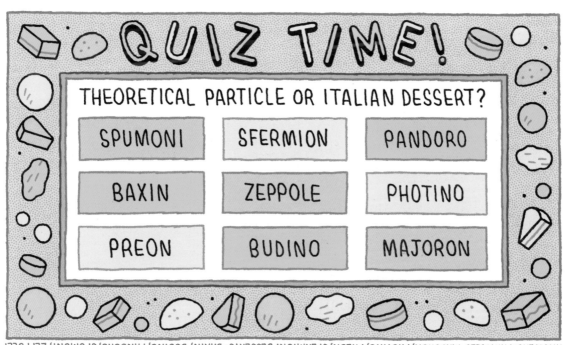

QUIZ TIME!
THEORETICAL PARTICLE OR ITALIAN DESSERT?
SPUMONI
SFERMION
PANDORO
BAXIN
ZEPPOLE
PHOTINO
PREON
BUDINO
MAJORON

ANSWERS. PARTICLES: MAJORON, PHOTINO, PREON, SFERMION. DESSERTS: BAXIN, BUDINO, PANDORO, SPUMONI, ZEPPOLE.

TEXT ABBREVIATIONS FOR MARINE BIOLOGISTS

WTF?

WHAT'S THAT FISH?

LOL!

LET'S OBSERVE LOBSTERS!

NSFW

NO SUCCESS FINDING WHALES

BRB

BUSY RESEARCHING BARNACLES

OMG!!

OUTSTANDING MARINE GASTROPODS!!

BTW

BEWARE THE WALRUS

ROFL!
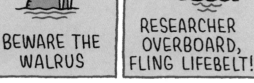
RESEARCHER OVERBOARD, FLING LIFEBELT!

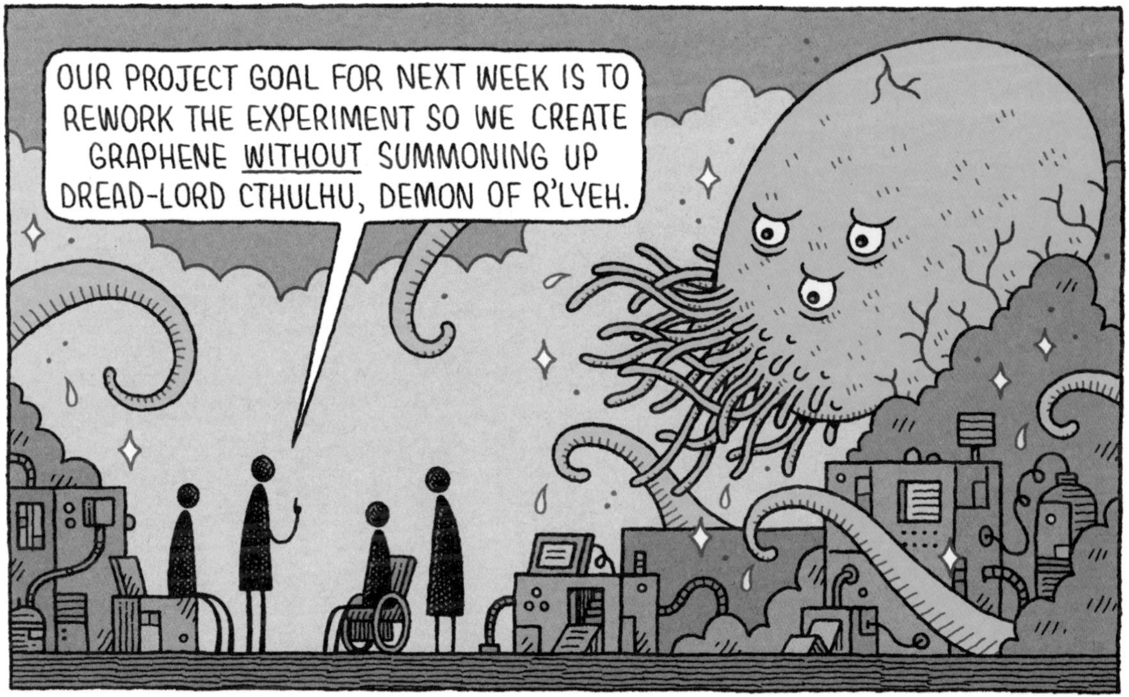
OUR PROJECT GOAL FOR NEXT WEEK IS TO REWORK THE EXPERIMENT SO WE CREATE GRAPHENE WITHOUT SUMMONING UP DREAD-LORD CTHULHU, DEMON OF R'LYEH.

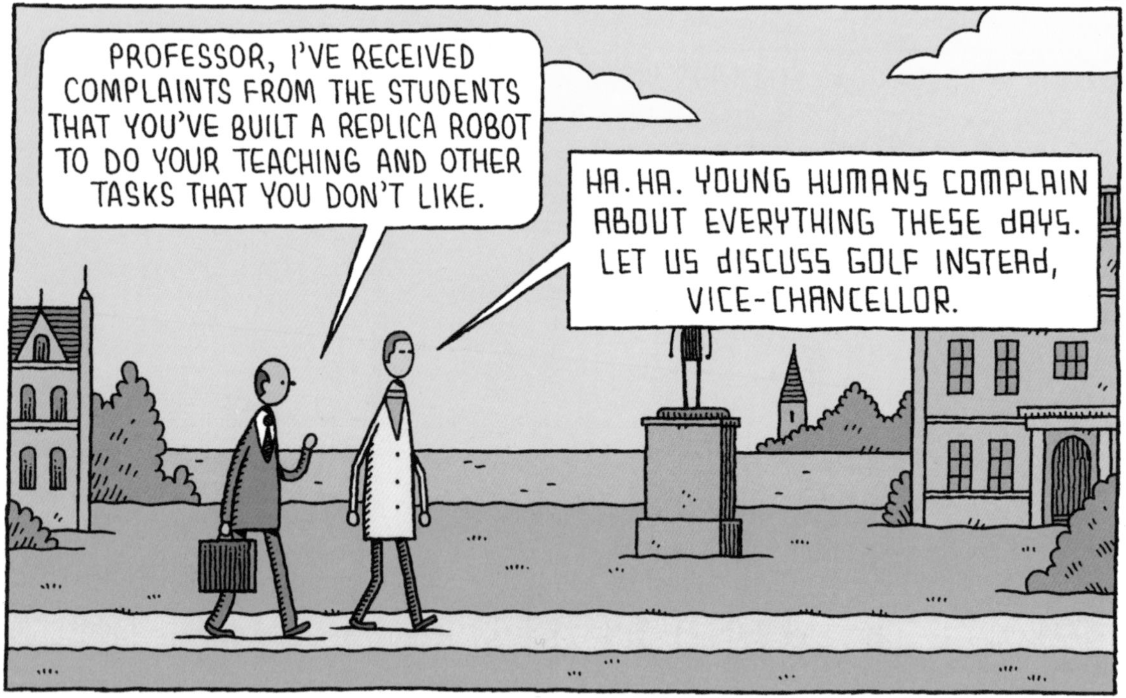
PROFESSOR, I'VE RECEIVED COMPLAINTS FROM THE STUDENTS THAT YOU'VE BUILT A REPLICA ROBOT TO DO YOUR TEACHING AND OTHER TASKS THAT YOU DON'T LIKE.
HA. HA. YOUNG HUMANS COMPLAIN ABOUT EVERYTHING THESE DAYS. LET US DISCUSS GOLF INSTEAD, VICE-CHANCELLOR.

MOON AND COMET

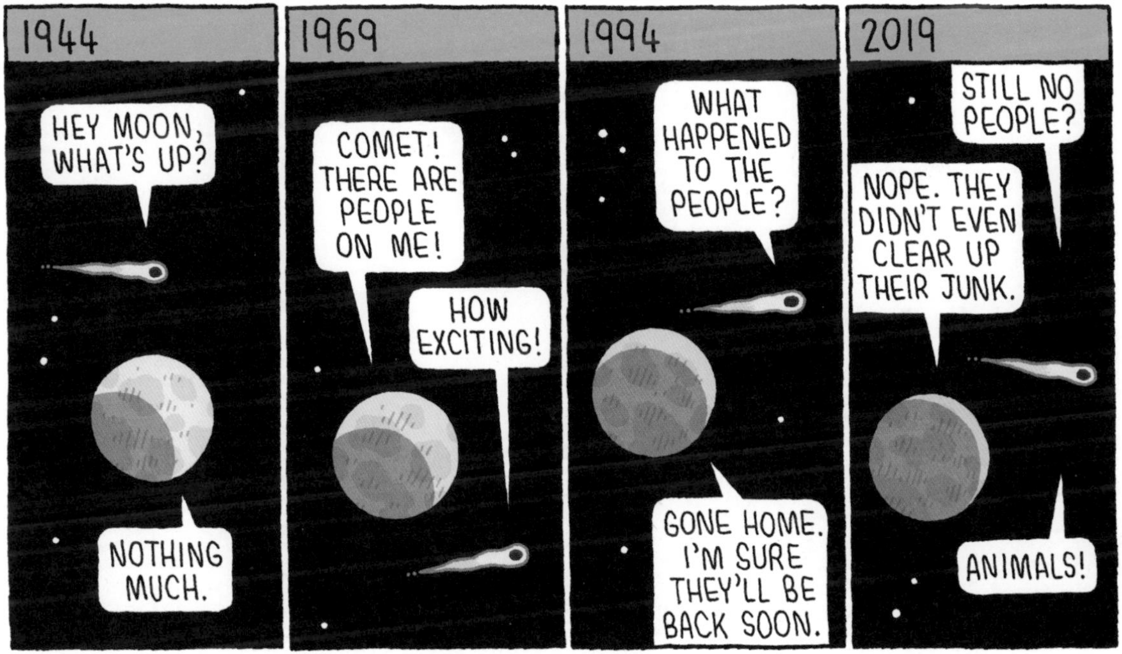

1944
HEY MOON, WHAT'S UP?
NOTHING MUCH.
1969
COMET! THERE ARE PEOPLE ON ME!
HOW EXCITING!
1994
WHAT HAPPENED TO THE PEOPLE?
GONE HOME. I'M SURE THEY'LL BE BACK SOON.
2019
STILL NO PEOPLE?
NOPE. THEY DIDN'T EVEN CLEAR UP THEIR JUNK.
ANIMALS!

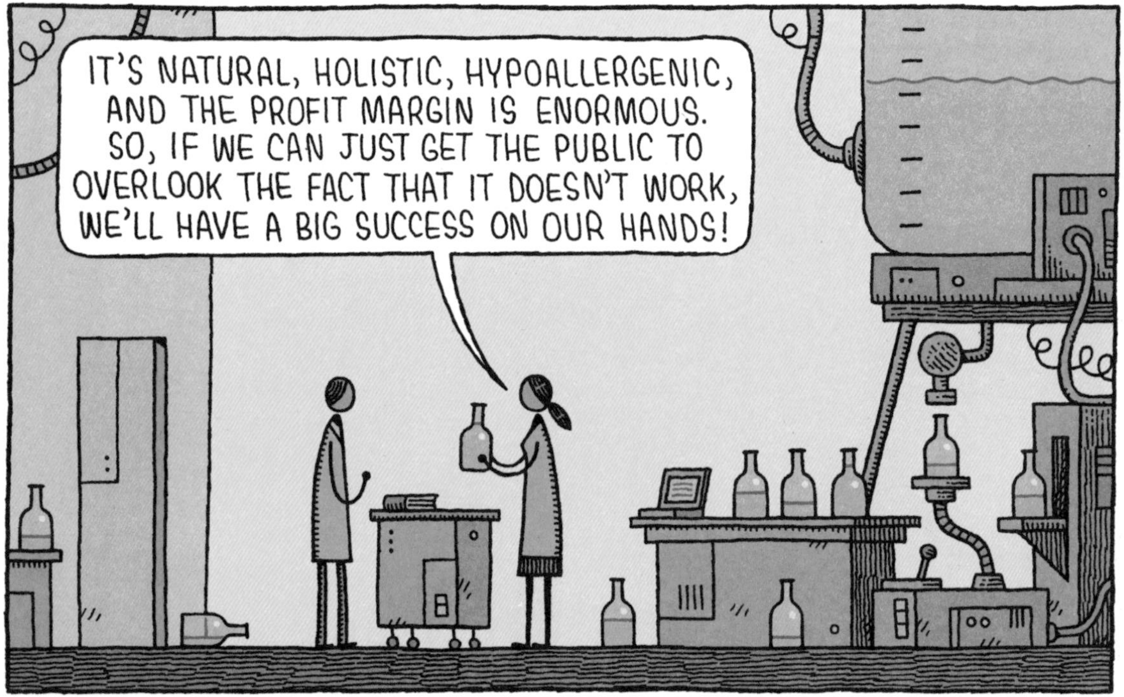
IT'S NATURAL, HOLISTIC, HYPOALLERGENIC, AND THE PROFIT MARGIN IS ENORMOUS. SO, IF WE CAN JUST GET THE PUBLIC TO OVERLOOK THE FACT THAT IT DOESN'T WORK, WE'LL HAVE A BIG SUCCESS ON OUR HANDS!

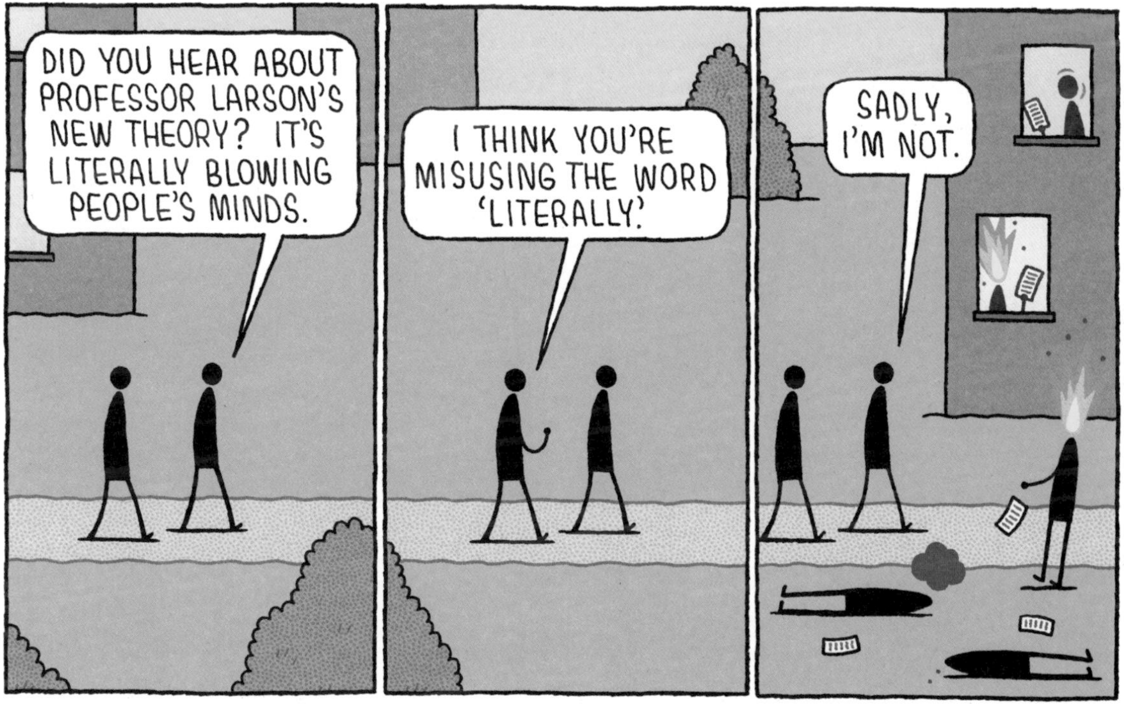
DID YOU HEAR ABOUT PROFESSOR LARSON'S NEW THEORY? IT'S LITERALLY BLOWING PEOPLE'S MINDS.
I THINK YOU'RE MISUSING THE WORD 'LITERALLY.'
SADLY, I'M NOT.

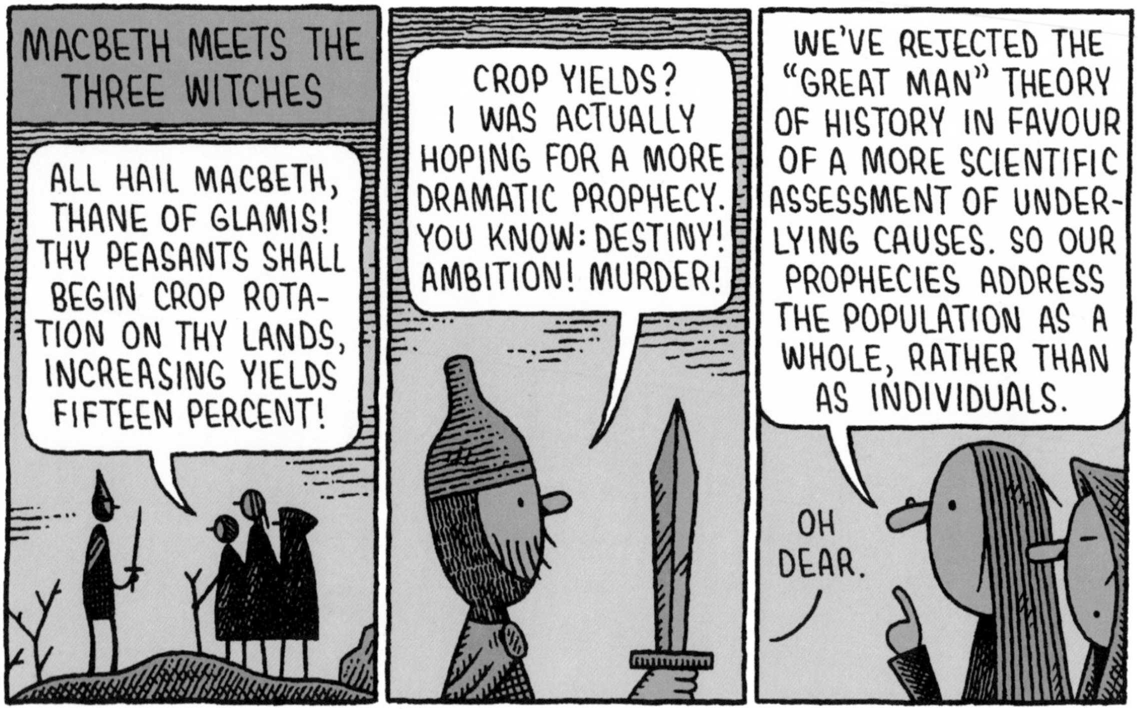
MACBETH MEETS THE THREE WITCHES
ALL HAIL MACBETH, THANE OF GLAMIS! THY PEASANTS SHALL BEGIN CROP ROTATION ON THY LANDS, INCREASING YIELDS FIFTEEN PERCENT!
CROP YIELDS? I WAS ACTUALLY HOPING FOR A MORE DRAMATIC PROPHECY. YOU KNOW: DESTINY! AMBITION! MURDER!
WE'VE REJECTED THE "GREAT MAN" THEORY OF HISTORY IN FAVOUR OF A MORE SCIENTIFIC ASSESSMENT OF UNDERLYING CAUSES. SO OUR PROPHECIES ADDRESS THE POPULATION AS A WHOLE, RATHER THAN AS INDIVIDUALS.
OH DEAR.

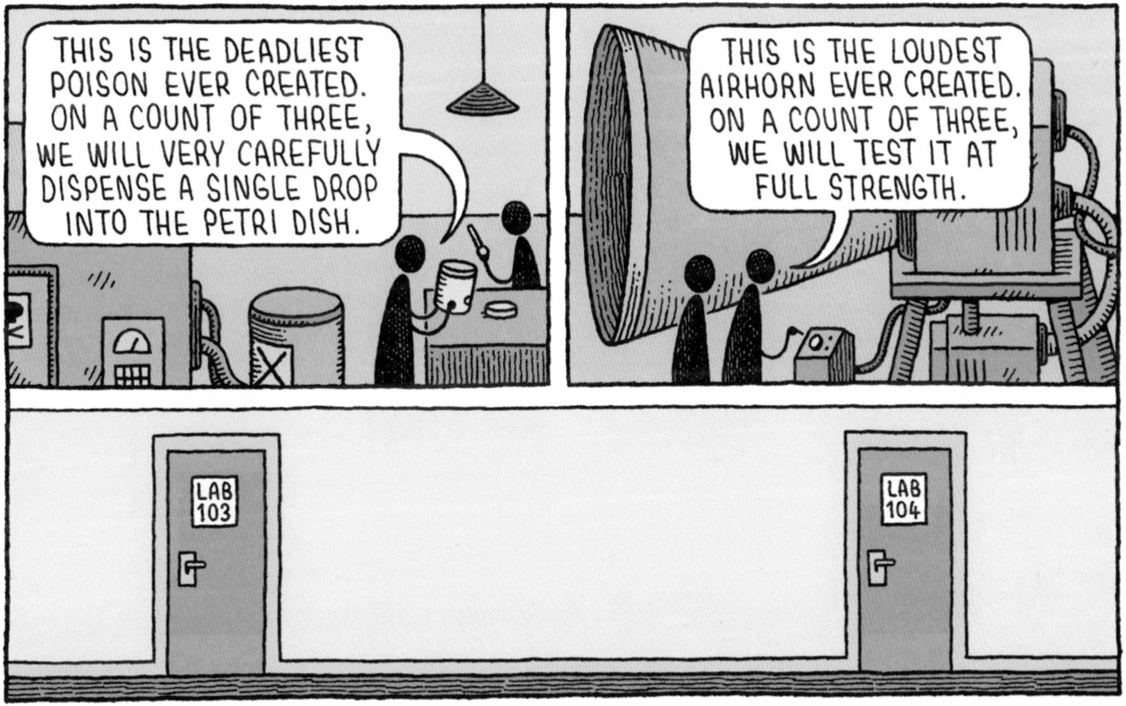
THIS IS THE DEADLIEST POISON EVER CREATED. ON A COUNT OF THREE, WE WILL VERY CAREFULLY DISPENSE A SINGLE DROP INTO THE PETRI DISH.
THIS IS THE LOUDEST AIRHORN EVER CREATED. ON A COUNT OF THREE, WE WILL TEST IT AT FULL STRENGTH.
LAB 103
LAB 104

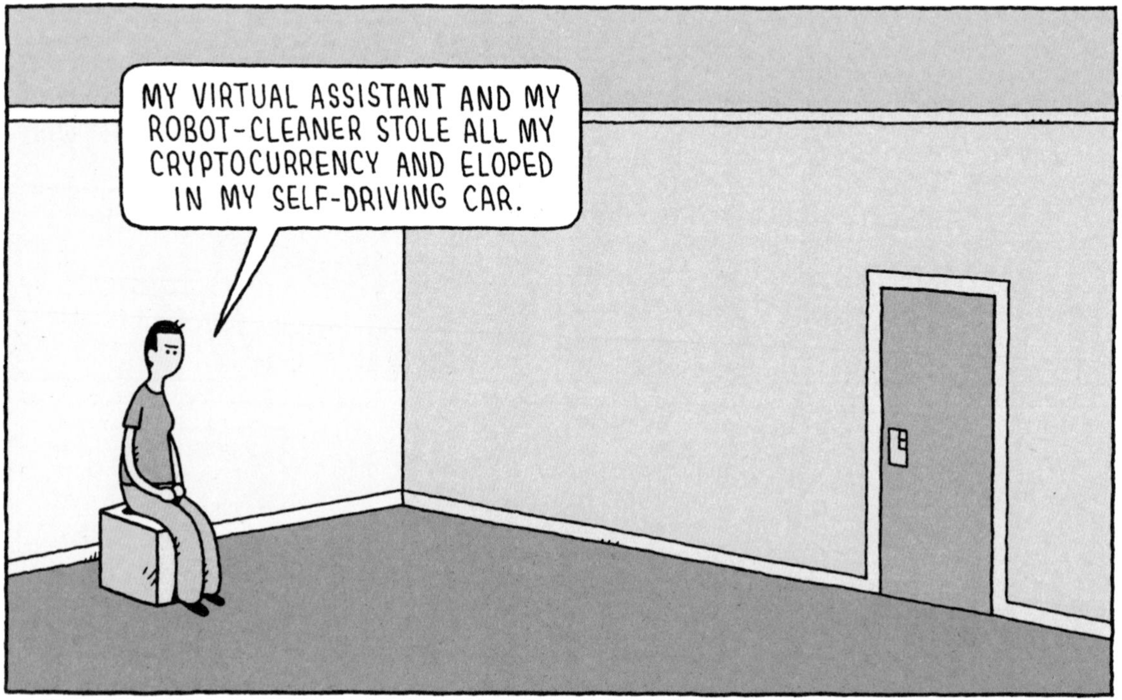
MY VIRTUAL ASSISTANT AND MY ROBOT-CLEANER STOLE ALL MY CRYPTOCURRENCY AND ELOPED IN MY SELF-DRIVING CAR.

NEW! CLASSIC FICTION WITH BINARY NUMBERS!

THE 11 MUSKETEERS
DUMAS
1100100 YEARS OF SOLITUDE
GARCÍA MÁRQUEZ
1100 ANGRY MEN
ROSE
CATCH-10110
HELLER
THE 100111 STEPS
BUCHAN
FAHRENHEIT 111000011
BRADBURY
A TALE OF 10 CITIES
DICKENS
THE 1100101 DALMATIANS
SMITH

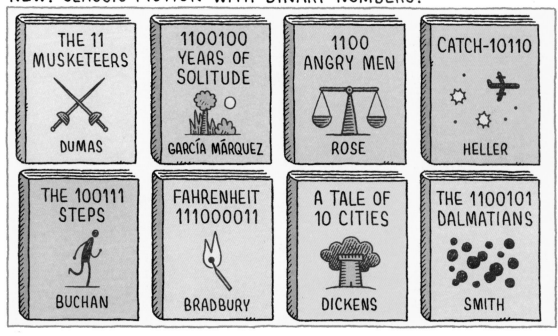

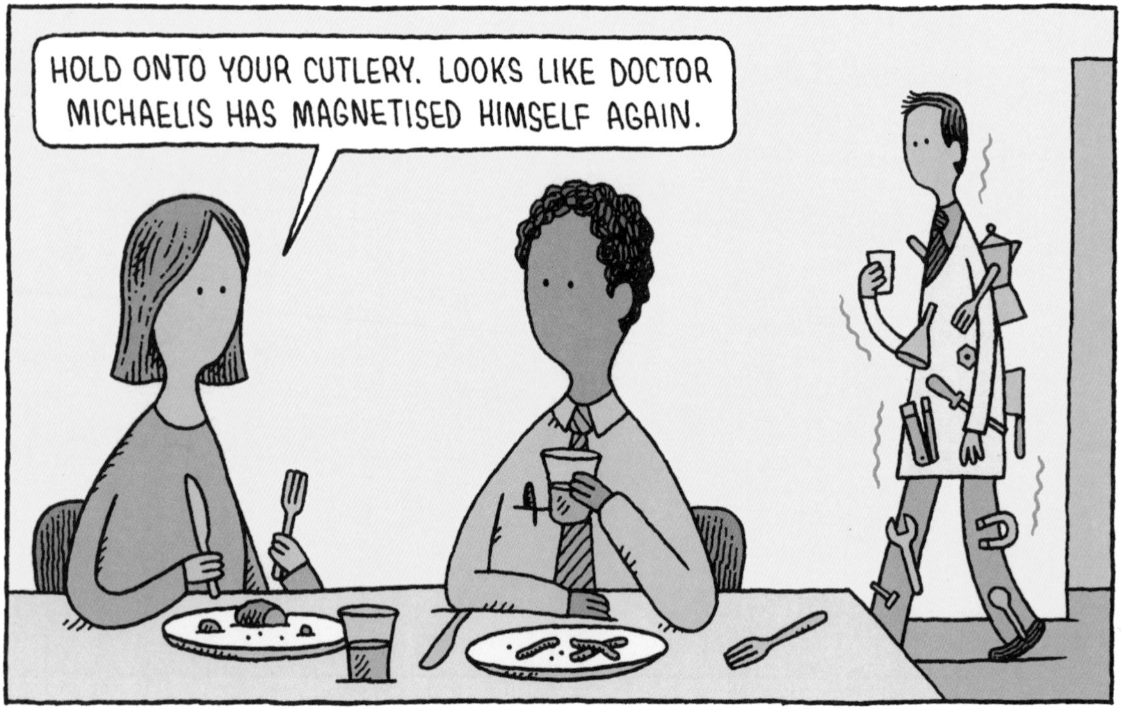
HOLD ONTO YOUR CUTLERY. LOOKS LIKE DOCTOR MICHAELIS HAS MAGNETISED HIMSELF AGAIN.

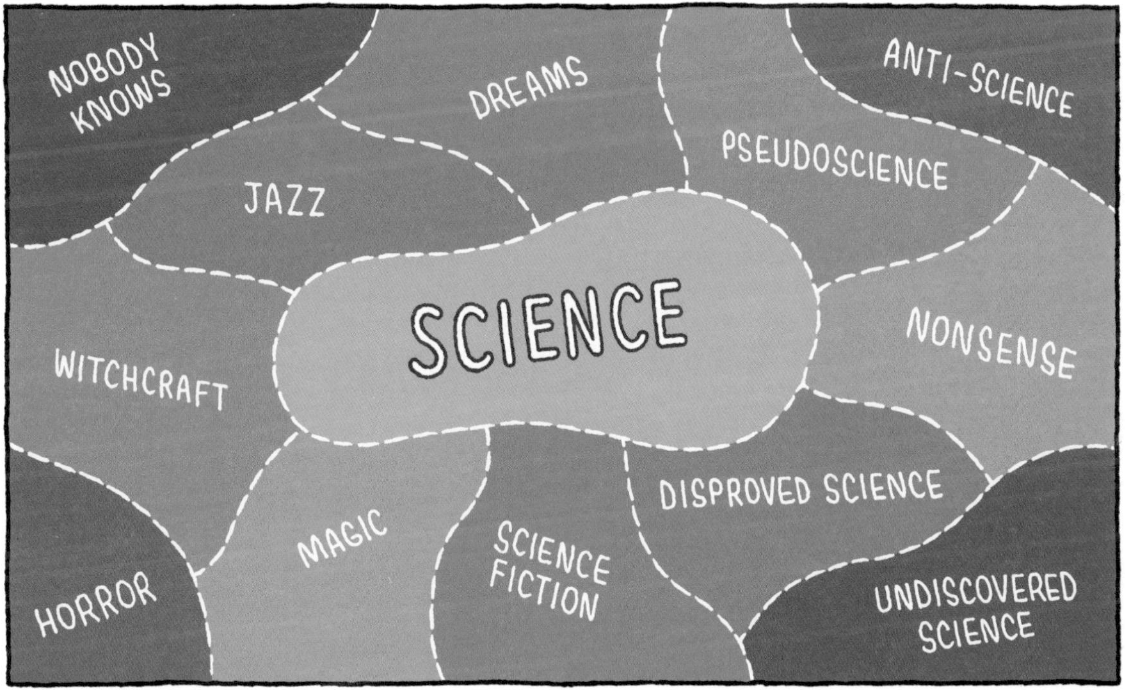
NOBODY KNOWS
DREAMS
ANTI-SCIENCE
PSEUDOSCIENCE
JAZZ
SCIENCE
WITCHCRAFT
NONSENSE
DISPROVED SCIENCE
MAGIC
SCIENCE FICTION
HORROR
UNDISCOVERED SCIENCE

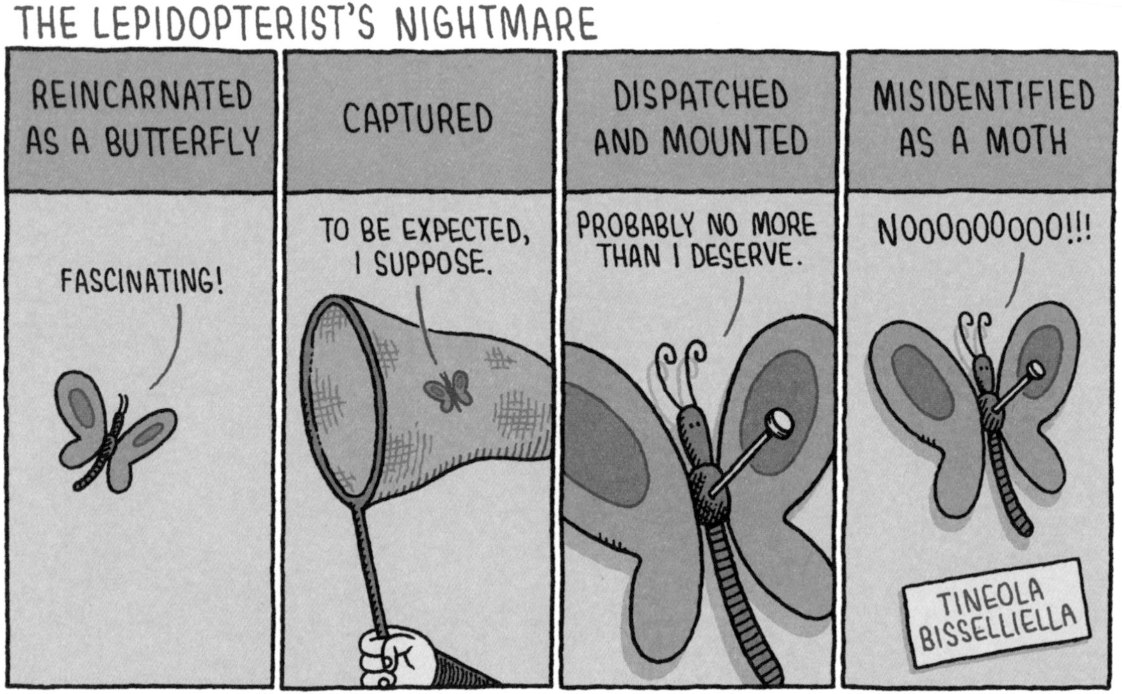
THE LEPIDOPTERIST'S NIGHTMARE
REINCARNATED AS A BUTTERFLY
FASCINATING!
CAPTURED
TO BE EXPECTED, I SUPPOSE.
DISPATCHED AND MOUNTED
PROBABLY NO MORE THAN I DESERVE.
MISIDENTIFIED AS A MOTH
NOOOOOOOOO!!!
TINEOLA BISSELLIELLA

NEWLY DISCOVERED NUMBERS:

CLONTY-THREE

A MEDIUM-SIZED ODD NUMBER THAT ONLY EXISTS AT THE CENTRE OF A BLACK HOLE.

STRAX

A RARE NUMBER THAT BEHAVES EXACTLY LIKE SEVEN, BUT WITH EXTRA GLAMOUR AND PIZZAZZ.

BLENTEEN

APPEARS BETWEEN 18 AND 17 WHEN COUNTING BACKWARDS BY THE LIGHT OF A FULL MOON.

FLERG

A DANGEROUSLY UNSTABLE PRIME NUMBER THAT EXPLODES WHEN MULTIPLIED.

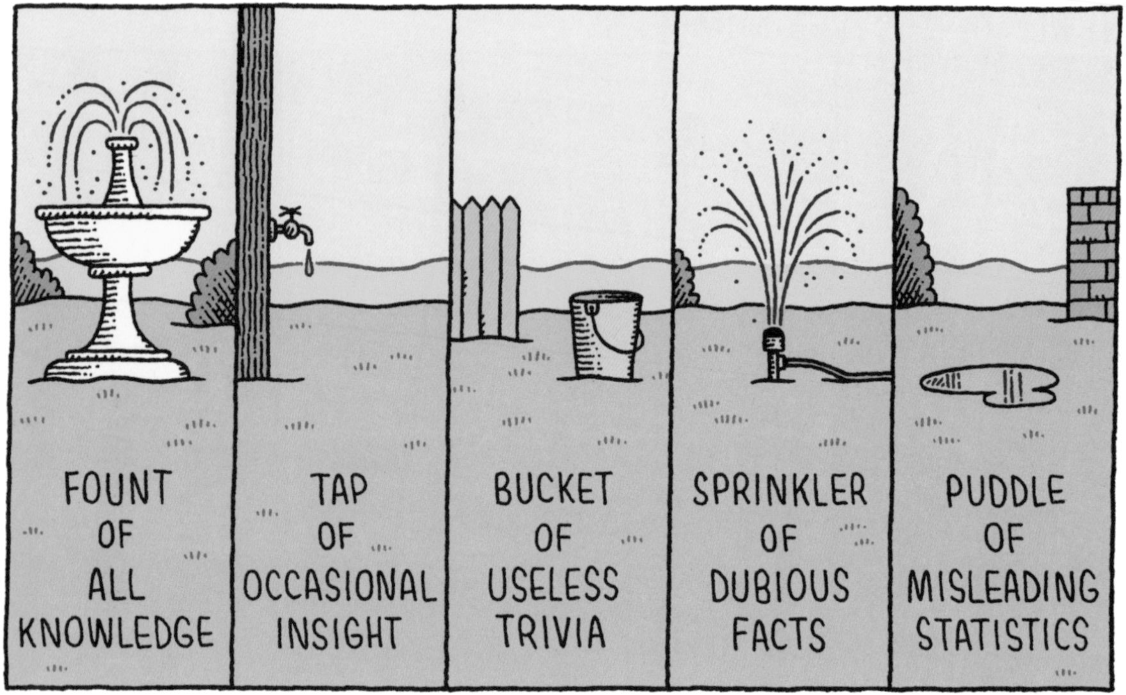
FOUNT OF ALL KNOWLEDGE
TAP OF OCCASIONAL INSIGHT
BUCKET OF USELESS TRIVIA
SPRINKLER OF DUBIOUS FACTS
PUDDLE OF MISLEADING STATISTICS

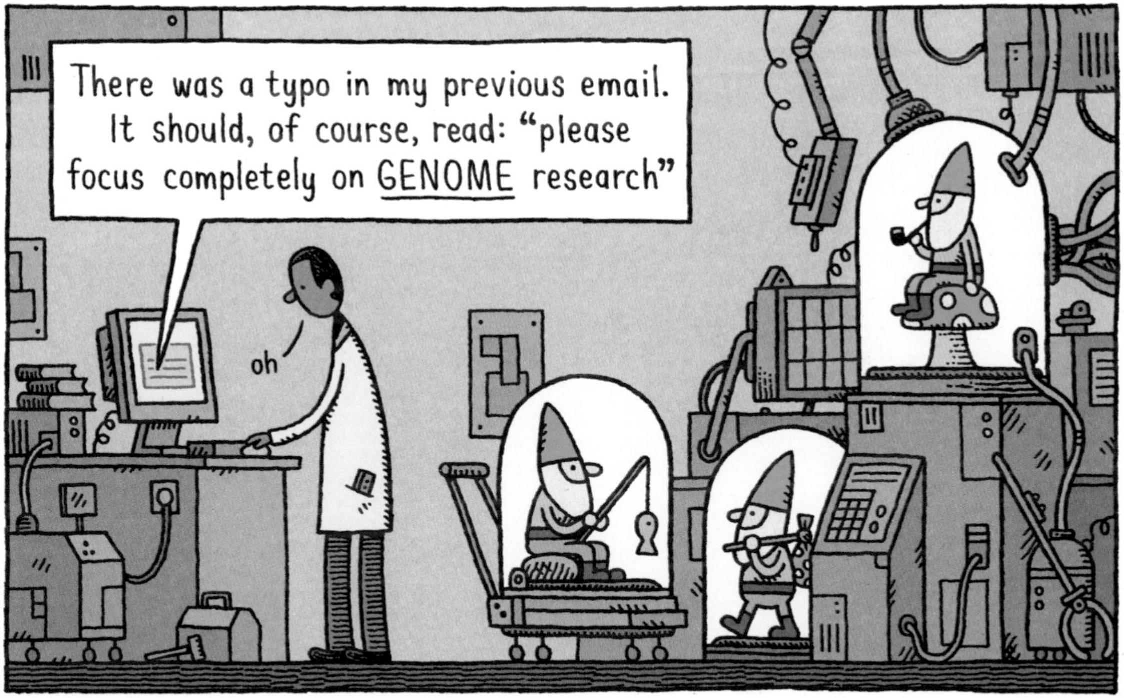
There was a typo in my previous email. It should, of course, read: "please focus completely on GENOME research"
oh

ANGRY PLANT

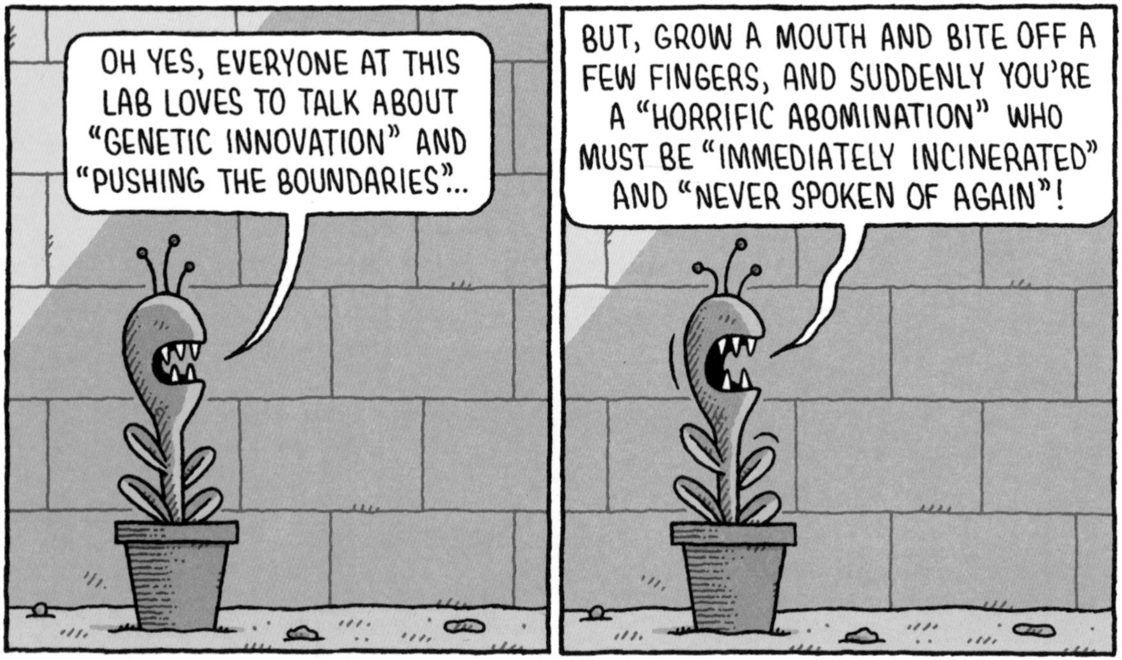
OH YES, EVERYONE AT THIS LAB LOVES TO TALK ABOUT "GENETIC INNOVATION" AND "PUSHING THE BOUNDARIES"...
BUT, GROW A MOUTH AND BITE OFF A FEW FINGERS, AND SUDDENLY YOU'RE A "HORRIFIC ABOMINATION" WHO MUST BE "IMMEDIATELY INCINERATED" AND "NEVER SPOKEN OF AGAIN"!

THE SPACE PROBE BEGINS ITS JOURNEY TO THE FURTHEST REACHES OF THE UNIVERSE.

THE SCIENTIST IS PARTICULARLY PROUD OF THE POEM THAT LIES WITHIN:

A PAEAN TO THE MAGIC OF EARTH, LIFE, AND THE COSMOS. COMMISSIONED FROM A GREAT POET AND PLACED WITHIN THE CRAFT BY THE SCIENTIST HERSELF, IN THE HOPE THAT IT MIGHT, ONE DAY, BE READ BY ANOTHER LIFEFORM.

THE DRY CLEANER SAYS THAT HE IS MOVED BY THE BEAUTIFUL WORDS, BUT WOULD PREFER THE RECEIPT FOR THE SCIENTIST'S CLOTHES.

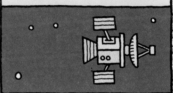

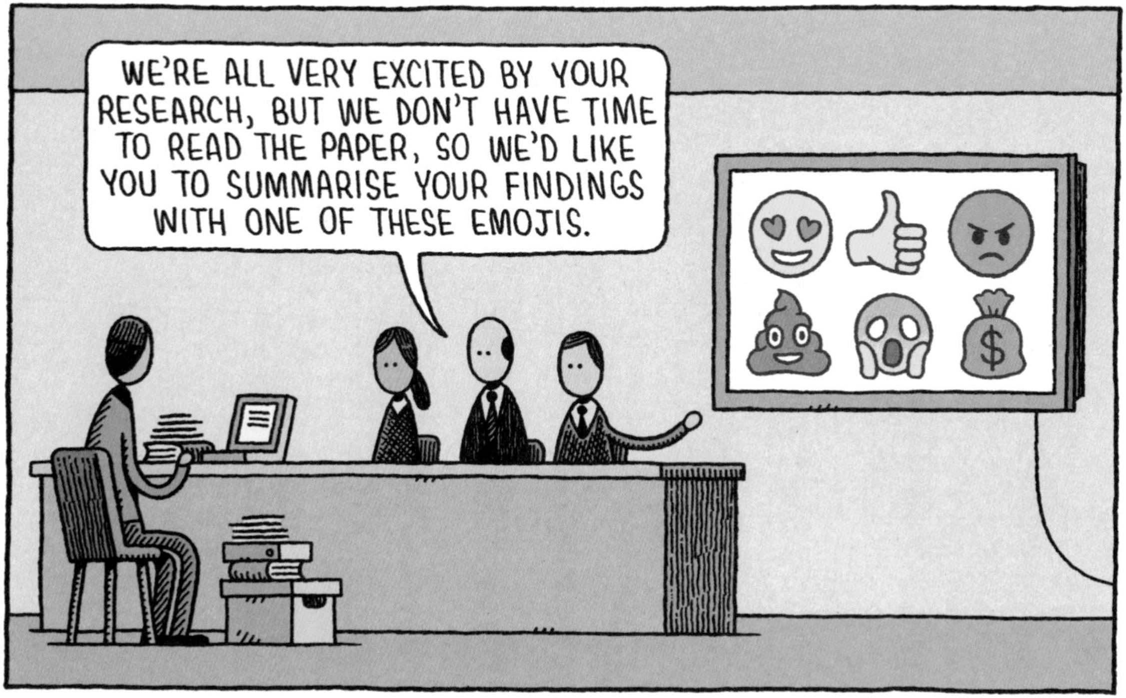
WE'RE ALL VERY EXCITED BY YOUR RESEARCH, BUT WE DON'T HAVE TIME TO READ THE PAPER, SO WE'D LIKE YOU TO SUMMARISE YOUR FINDINGS WITH ONE OF THESE EMOJIS.
$

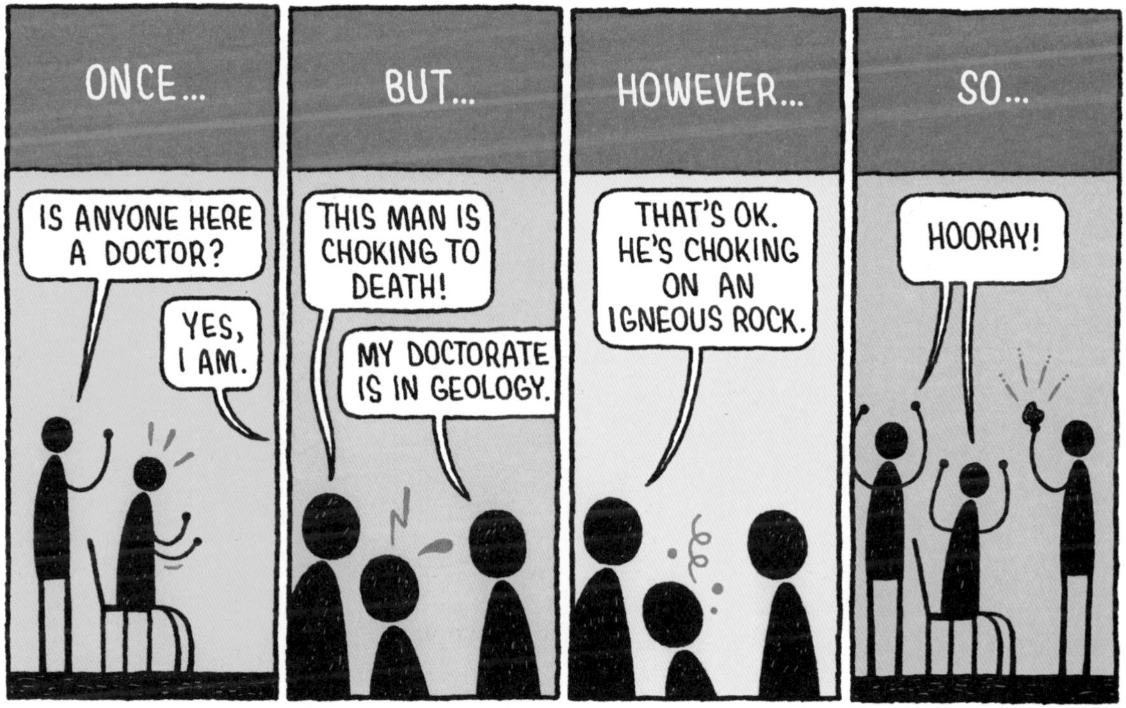
ONCE...
IS ANYONE HERE A DOCTOR?
YES, I AM.
BUT...
THIS MAN IS CHOKING TO DEATH!
MY DOCTORATE IS IN GEOLOGY.
HOWEVER...
THAT'S OK. HE'S CHOKING ON AN IGNEOUS ROCK.
SO...
HOORAY!

THE DEVICE

THE EXPERIMENT TAKES A PAIR OF TWINS.

ONE CONTINUES HER LIFE WITH NO CHANGES.

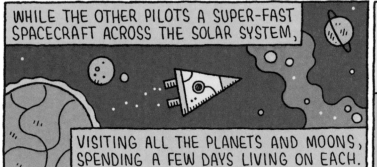

WHILE THE OTHER PILOTS A SUPER-FAST SPACECRAFT ACROSS THE SOLAR SYSTEM,

VISITING ALL THE PLANETS AND MOONS, SPENDING A FEW DAYS LIVING ON EACH.

WHEN THE ASTRONAUT RETURNS, THE DEVICE IS USED TO MEASURE HOW JEALOUS HER SISTER IS.

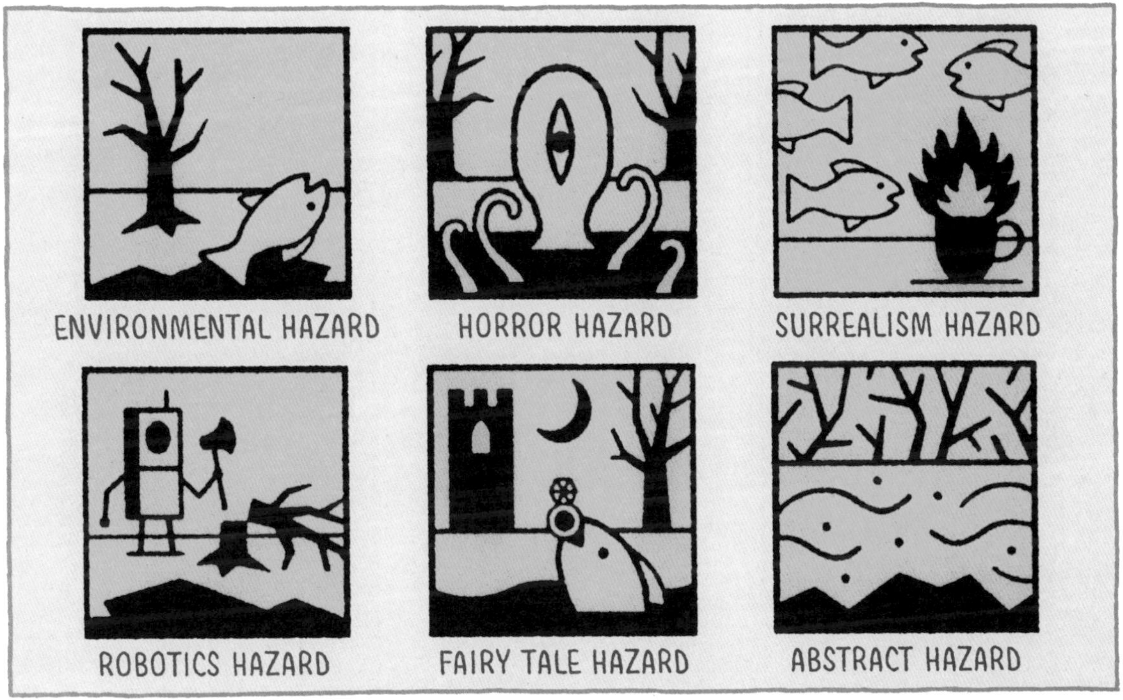
ENVIRONMENTAL HAZARD
HORROR HAZARD
SURREALISM HAZARD
ROBOTICS HAZARD
FAIRY TALE HAZARD
ABSTRACT HAZARD

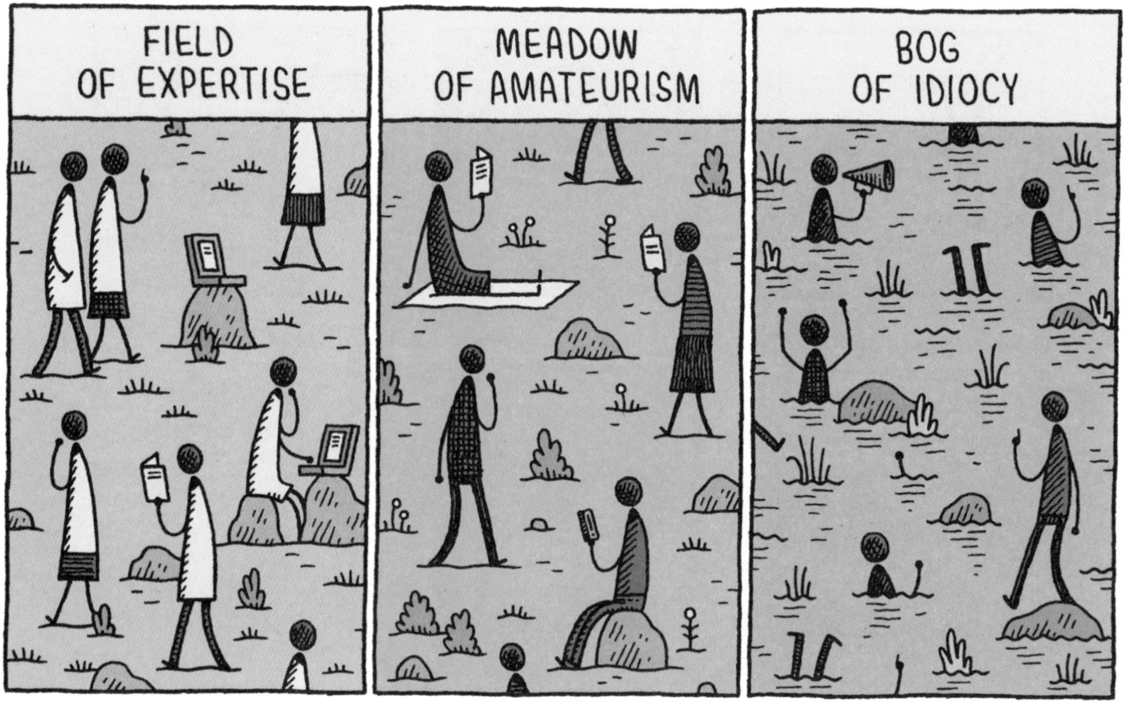
FIELD OF EXPERTISE
MEADOW OF AMATEURISM
BOG OF IDIOCY

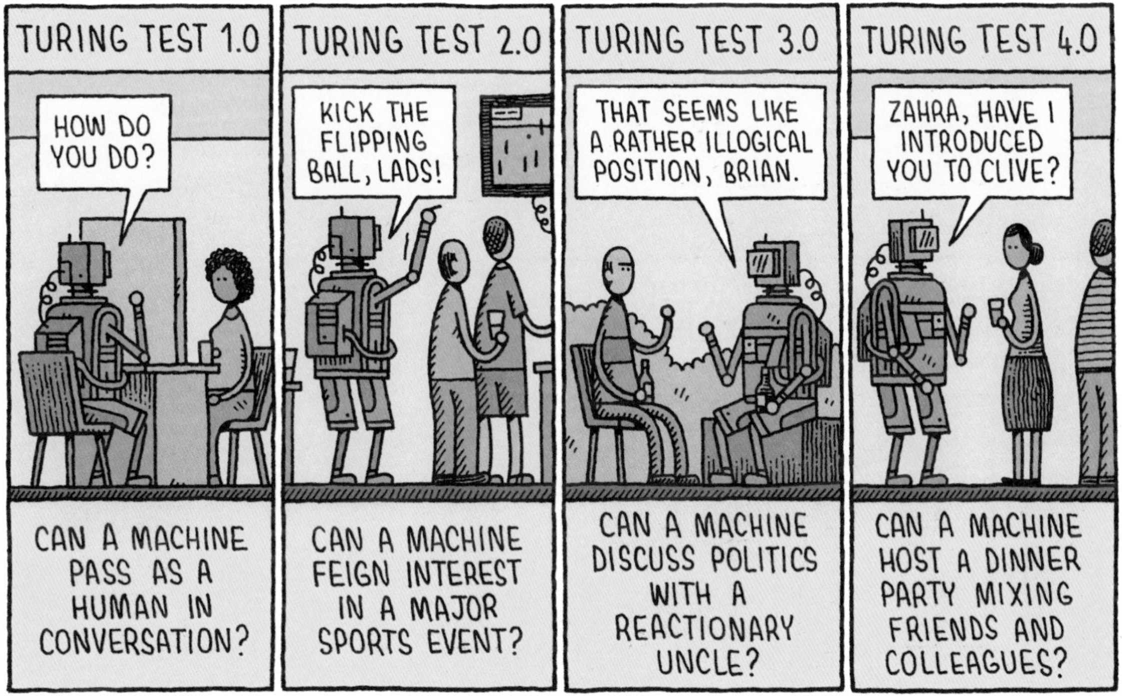
TURING TEST 1.0
HOW DO YOU DO?
CAN A MACHINE PASS AS A HUMAN IN CONVERSATION?
TURING TEST 2.0
KICK THE FLIPPING BALL, LADS!
CAN A MACHINE FEIGN INTEREST IN A MAJOR SPORTS EVENT?
TURING TEST 3.0
THAT SEEMS LIKE A RATHER ILLOGICAL POSITION, BRIAN.
CAN A MACHINE DISCUSS POLITICS WITH A REACTIONARY UNCLE?
TURING TEST 4.0
ZAHRA, HAVE I INTRODUCED YOU TO CLIVE?
CAN A MACHINE HOST A DINNER PARTY MIXING FRIENDS AND COLLEAGUES?

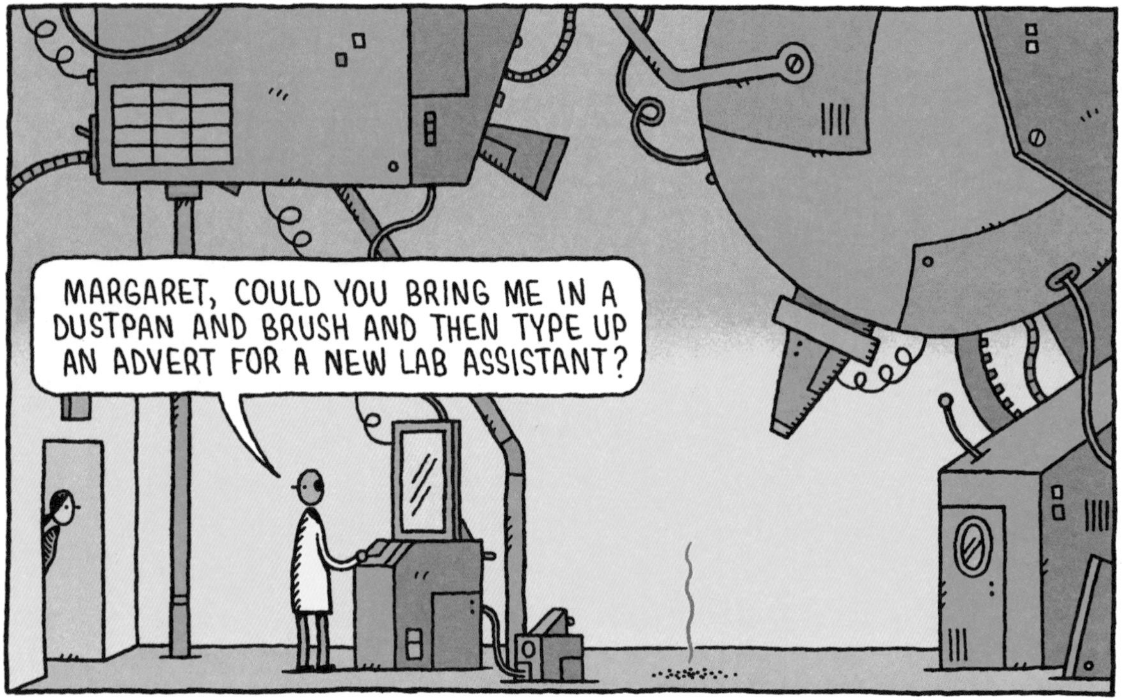
MARGARET, COULD YOU BRING ME IN A DUSTPAN AND BRUSH AND THEN TYPE UP AN ADVERT FOR A NEW LAB ASSISTANT?

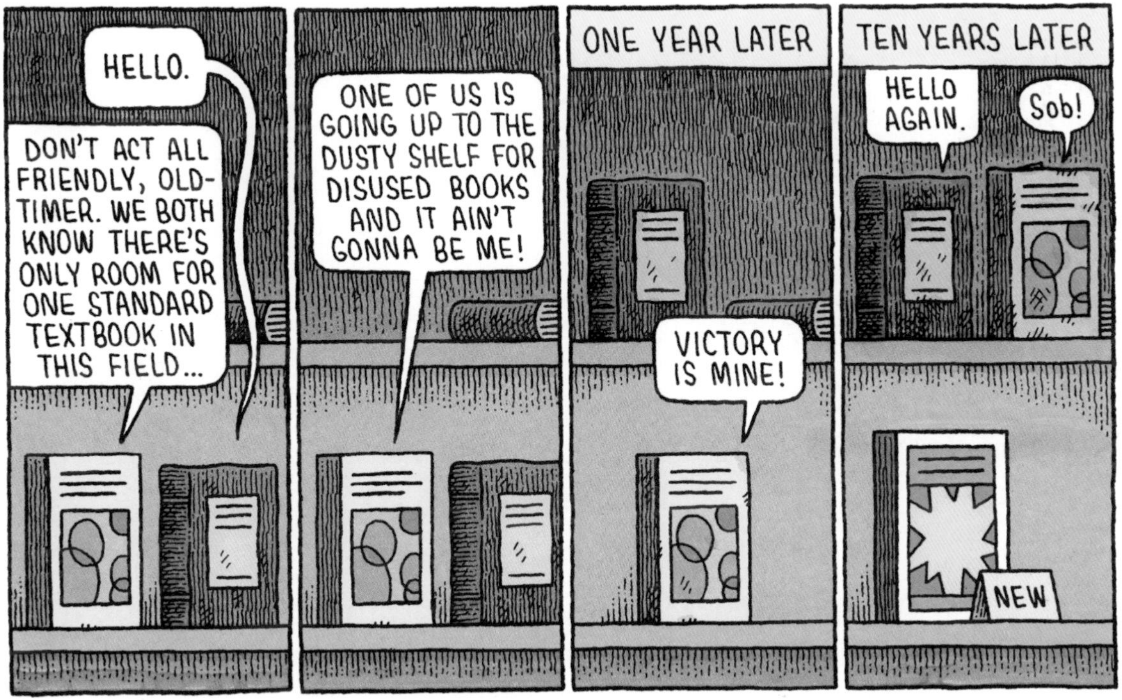
HELLO.
DON'T ACT ALL FRIENDLY, OLD-TIMER. WE BOTH KNOW THERE'S ONLY ROOM FOR ONE STANDARD TEXTBOOK IN THIS FIELD...
ONE OF US IS GOING UP TO THE DUSTY SHELF FOR DISUSED BOOKS AND IT AIN'T GONNA BE ME!
ONE YEAR LATER
VICTORY IS MINE!
TEN YEARS LATER
HELLO AGAIN.
Sob!
NEW

UPON ENCOUNTERING A POWERFUL RIVAL, DOCTOR WILLIAMS, INSPIRED BY THE CEPHALOPODS SHE IS STUDYING, RELEASES A LARGE QUANTITY OF BLACK INK AND MAKES A RAPID RETREAT.

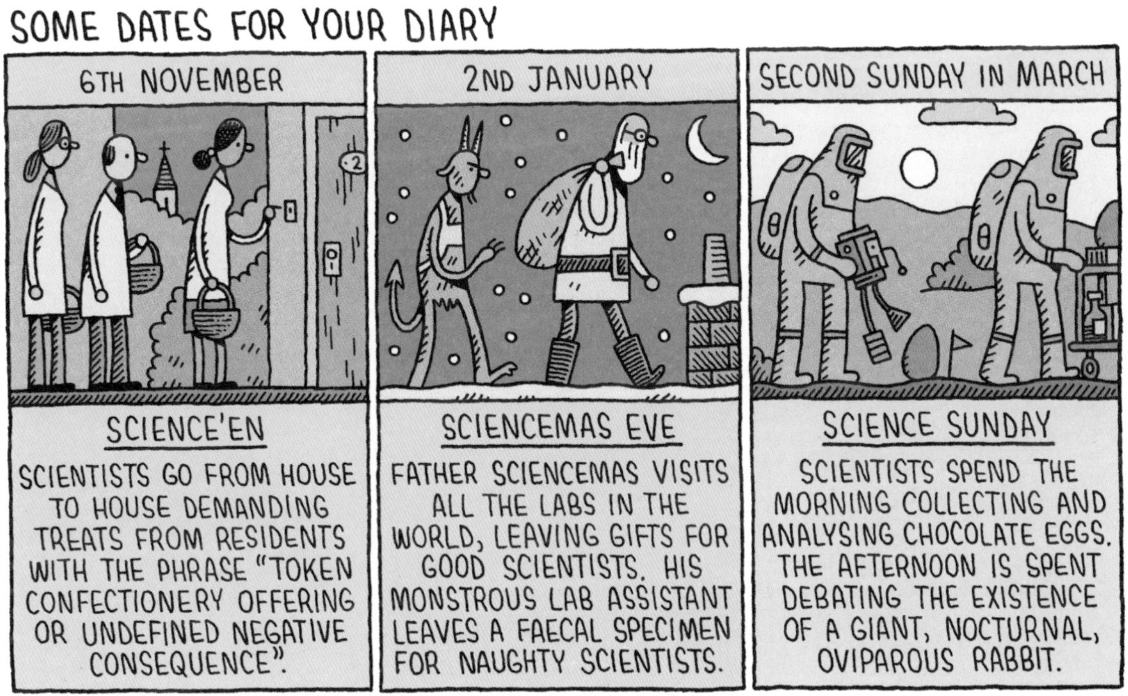
SOME DATES FOR YOUR DIARY
6TH NOVEMBER
SCIENCE'EN
SCIENTISTS GO FROM HOUSE TO HOUSE DEMANDING TREATS FROM RESIDENTS WITH THE PHRASE "TOKEN CONFECTIONERY OFFERING OR UNDEFINED NEGATIVE CONSEQUENCE".
2ND JANUARY
SCIENCEMAS EVE
FATHER SCIENCEMAS VISITS ALL THE LABS IN THE WORLD, LEAVING GIFTS FOR GOOD SCIENTISTS. HIS MONSTROUS LAB ASSISTANT LEAVES A FAECAL SPECIMEN FOR NAUGHTY SCIENTISTS.
SECOND SUNDAY IN MARCH
SCIENCE SUNDAY
SCIENTISTS SPEND THE MORNING COLLECTING AND ANALYSING CHOCOLATE EGGS. THE AFTERNOON IS SPENT DEBATING THE EXISTENCE OF A GIANT, NOCTURNAL, OVIPAROUS RABBIT.

PRESENTING MY FINDINGS WITH INFOGRAPHICS

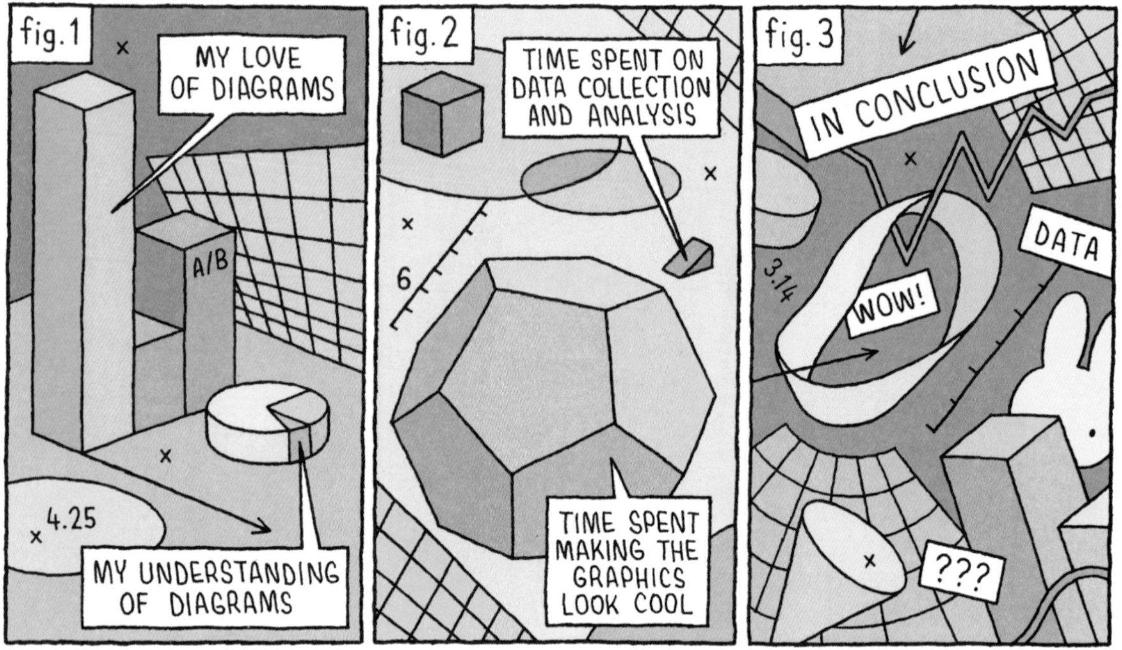
fig. 1
MY LOVE OF DIAGRAMS
A/B
4.25
MY UNDERSTANDING OF DIAGRAMS
fig. 2
TIME SPENT ON DATA COLLECTION AND ANALYSIS
6
TIME SPENT MAKING THE GRAPHICS LOOK COOL
fig. 3
IN CONCLUSION
DATA
3.14
WOW!
???

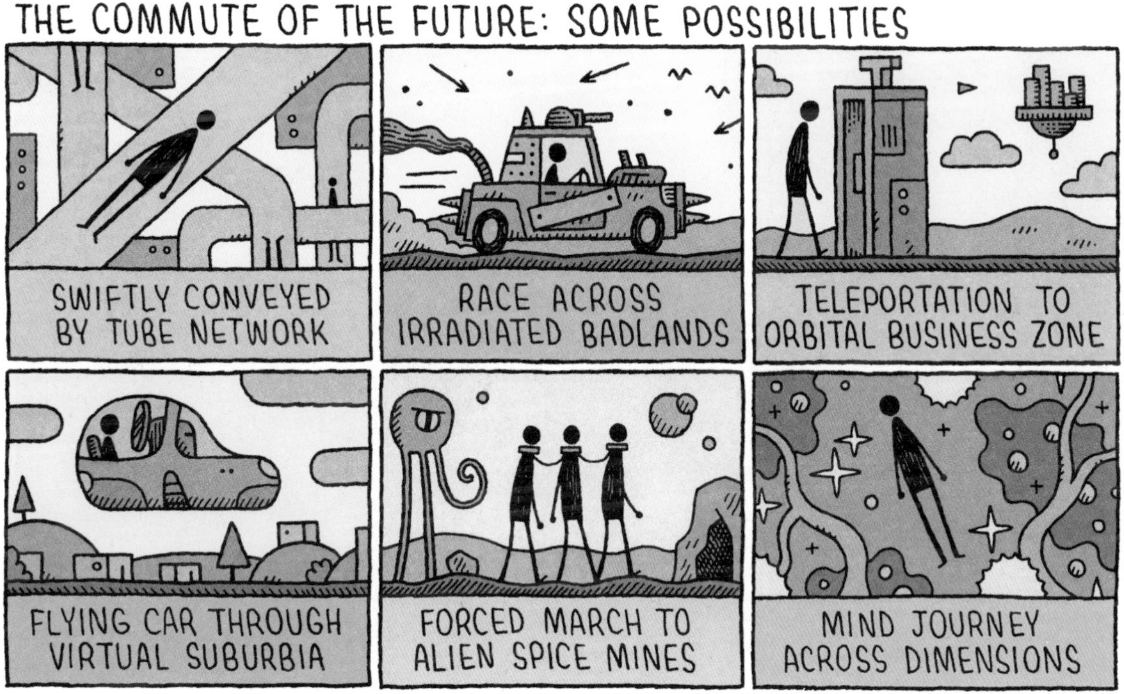
THE COMMUTE OF THE FUTURE: SOME POSSIBILITIES
SWIFTLY CONVEYED BY TUBE NETWORK
RACE ACROSS IRRADIATED BADLANDS
TELEPORTATION TO ORBITAL BUSINESS ZONE
FLYING CAR THROUGH VIRTUAL SUBURBIA
FORCED MARCH TO ALIEN SPICE MINES
MIND JOURNEY ACROSS DIMENSIONS

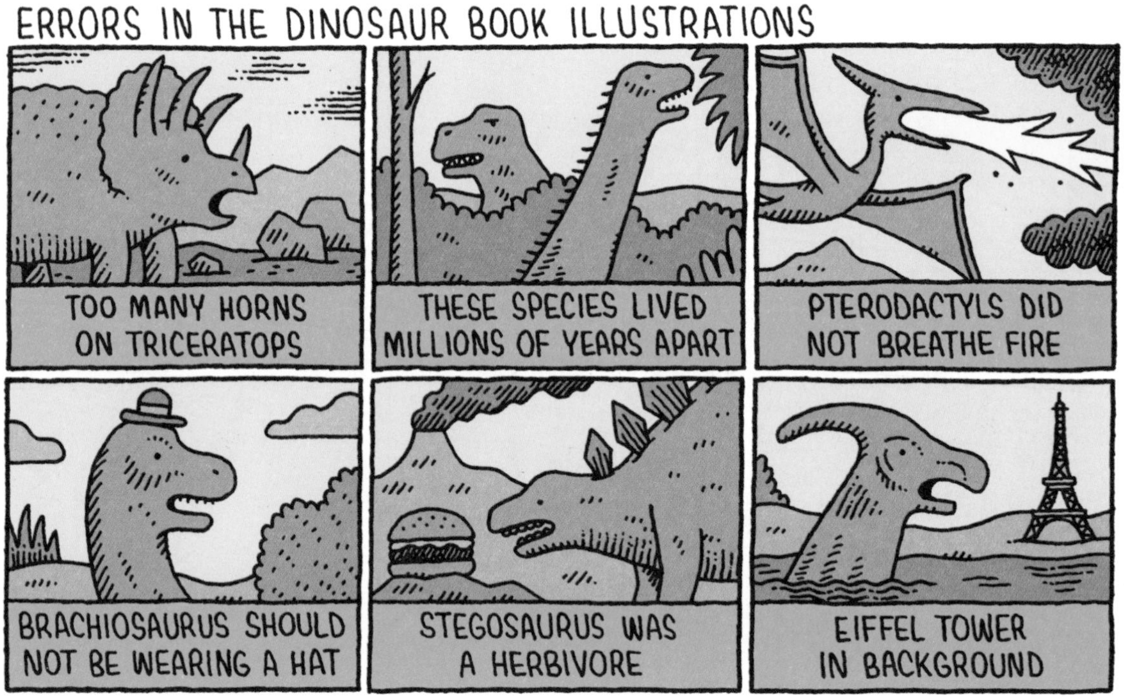
ERRORS IN THE DINOSAUR BOOK ILLUSTRATIONS
TOO MANY HORNS ON TRICERATOPS
THESE SPECIES LIVED MILLIONS OF YEARS APART
PTERODACTYLS DID NOT BREATHE FIRE
BRACHIOSAURUS SHOULD NOT BE WEARING A HAT
STEGOSAURUS WAS A HERBIVORE
EIFFEL TOWER IN BACKGROUND

THE EVIL SCIENTIST'S NOTES FOR THE PRESS CONFERENCE

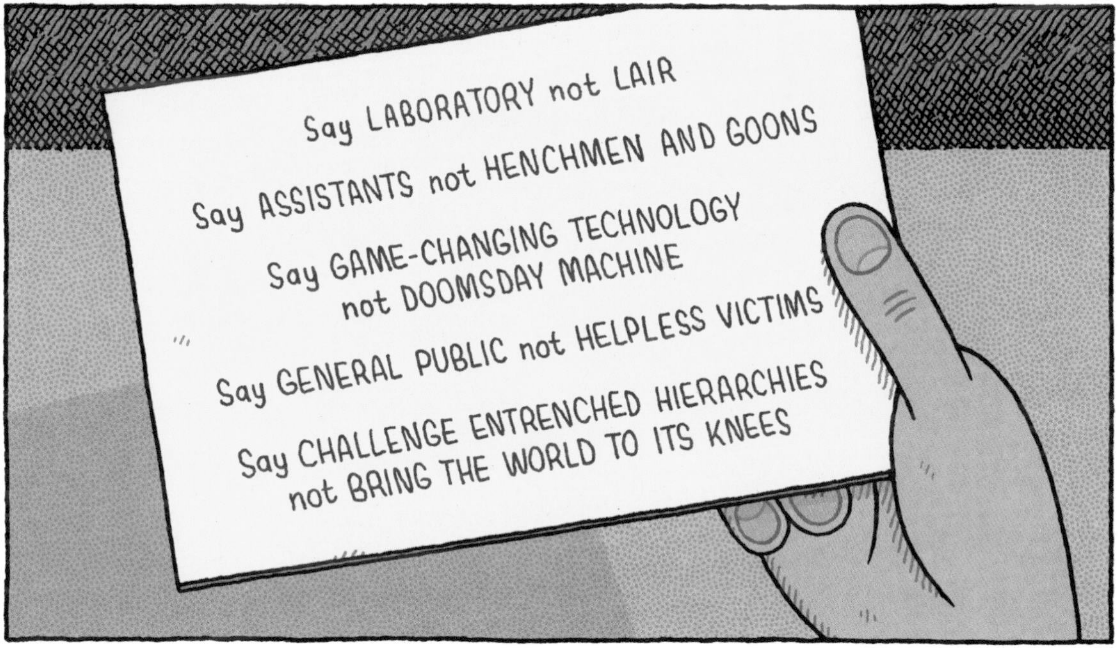
Say LABORATORY not LAIR
Say ASSISTANTS not HENCHMEN AND GOONS
Say GAME-CHANGING TECHNOLOGY not DOOMSDAY MACHINE
Say GENERAL PUBLIC not HELPLESS VICTIMS
Say CHALLENGE ENTRENCHED HIERARCHIES not BRING THE WORLD TO ITS KNEES

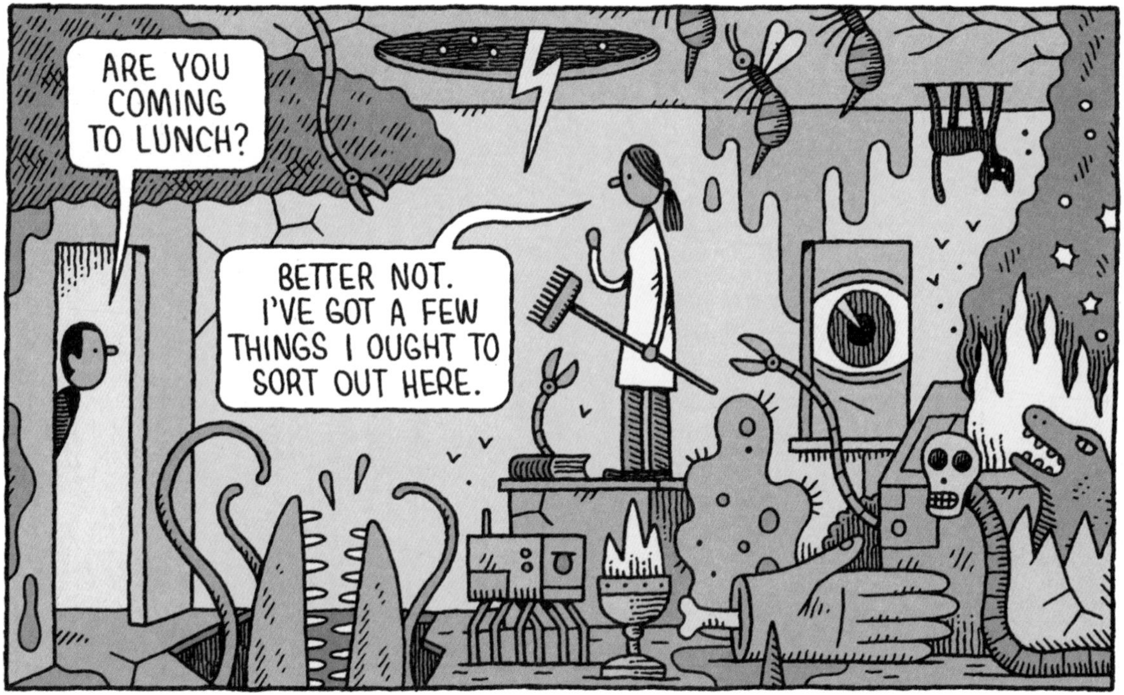
ARE YOU COMING TO LUNCH?
BETTER NOT. I'VE GOT A FEW THINGS I OUGHT TO SORT OUT HERE.

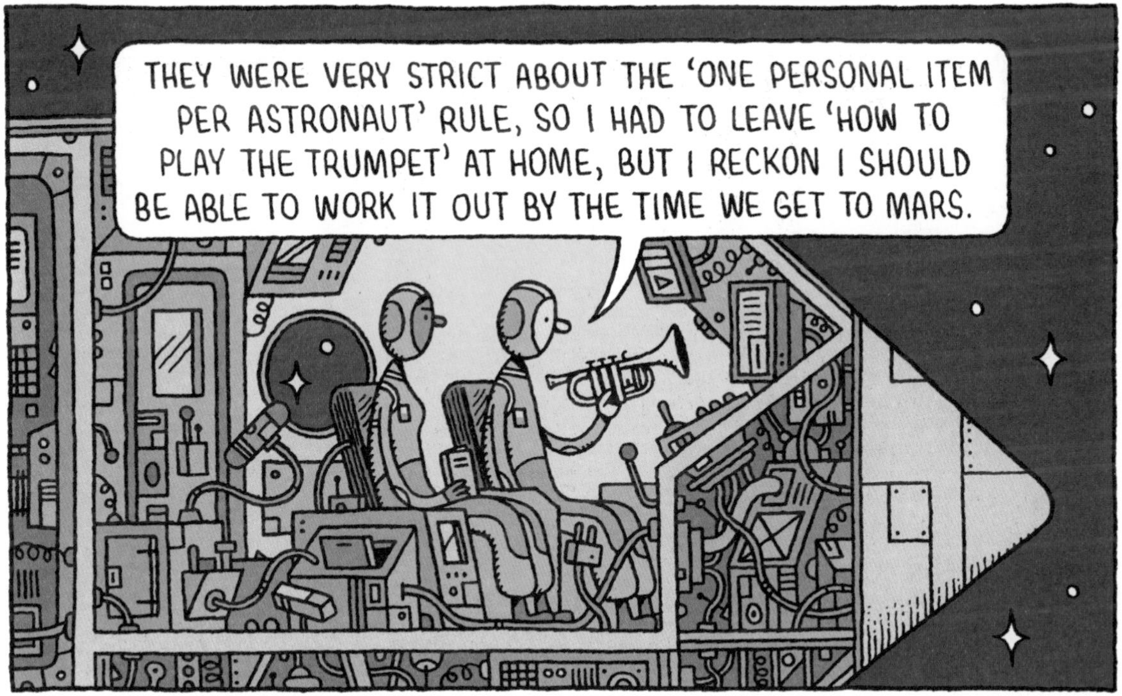
THEY WERE VERY STRICT ABOUT THE 'ONE PERSONAL ITEM PER ASTRONAUT' RULE, SO I HAD TO LEAVE 'HOW TO PLAY THE TRUMPET' AT HOME, BUT I RECKON I SHOULD BE ABLE TO WORK IT OUT BY THE TIME WE GET TO MARS.

MOTIVATIONAL POSTERS FOR SCIENTISTS

FOLLOW YOUR DREAMS

IN A RIGOROUSLY LOGICAL AND METICULOUSLY DETAILED MANNER, WITHIN CLEARLY DEFINED PARAMETERS

BELIEVE IN YOURSELF

UNLESS A COMPREHENSIVE ANALYSIS OF THE EVIDENCE LEADS YOU TO BELIEVE IN SOMETHING ELSE

LISTEN TO YOUR HEART

BUT ONLY FOLLOW ITS ADVICE IF IT STANDS UP TO THOROUGH INVESTIGATION AND REPEATED TESTING

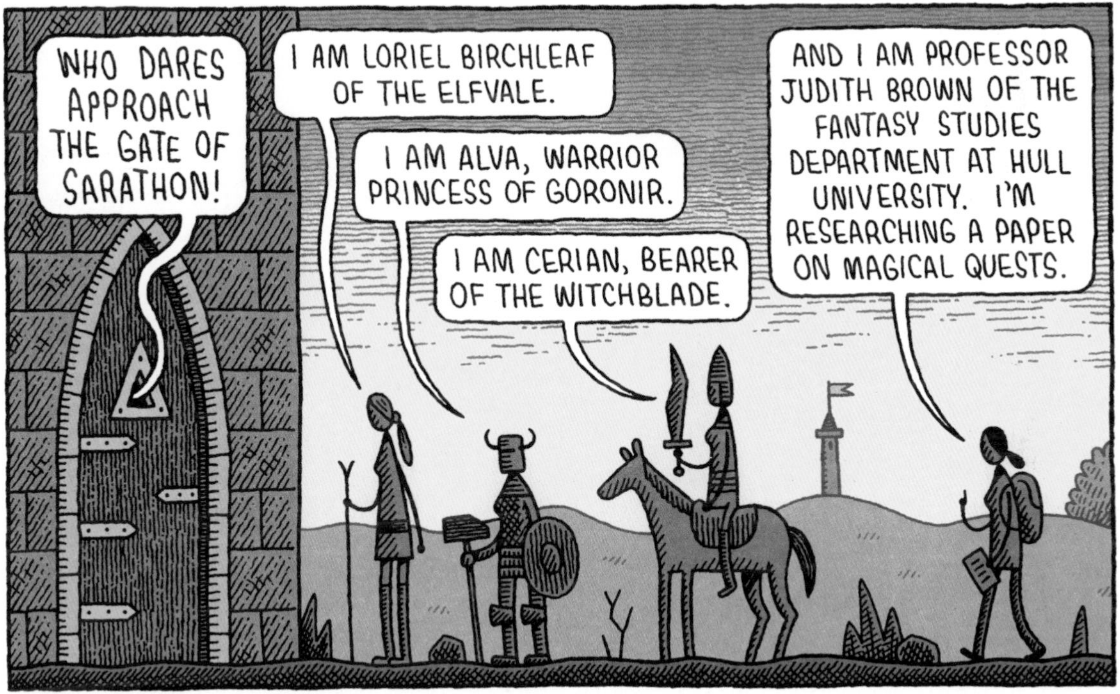
WHO DARES APPROACH THE GATE OF SARATHON!
I AM LORIEL BIRCHLEAF OF THE ELFVALE.
I AM ALVA, WARRIOR PRINCESS OF GORONIR.
I AM CERIAN, BEARER OF THE WITCHBLADE.
AND I AM PROFESSOR JUDITH BROWN OF THE FANTASY STUDIES DEPARTMENT AT HULL UNIVERSITY. I'M RESEARCHING A PAPER ON MAGICAL QUESTS.

FAKE NOBEL PRIZE SCAMS AND HOW TO AVOID THEM

NOBEL PRIZES FOR THE SCIENCES ARE PRESENTED BY THE KING OF SWEDEN. IF YOU ARE GIVEN A NOBEL PRIZE BY ANYBODY ELSE, IT WILL ALMOST CERTAINLY BE A FAKE.

ALFRED NOBEL DID NOT LEAVE A "SECRET CACHE OF SPARE NOBEL PRIZES IN A LONG-FORGOTTEN SWISS BANK VAULT" AND ANYONE CLAIMING TO HAVE ACCESS TO IT IS A FRAUDSTER.

THE OFFICIAL WEBSITE FOR NOBEL PRIZES IS NOBELPRIZE.ORG. BEWARE OF FAKE SITES SUCH AS YOUVEWONANOBEL.SE, BIGSCIENCECASHPRIZE.NET, AND NOBEL4U.BIZ

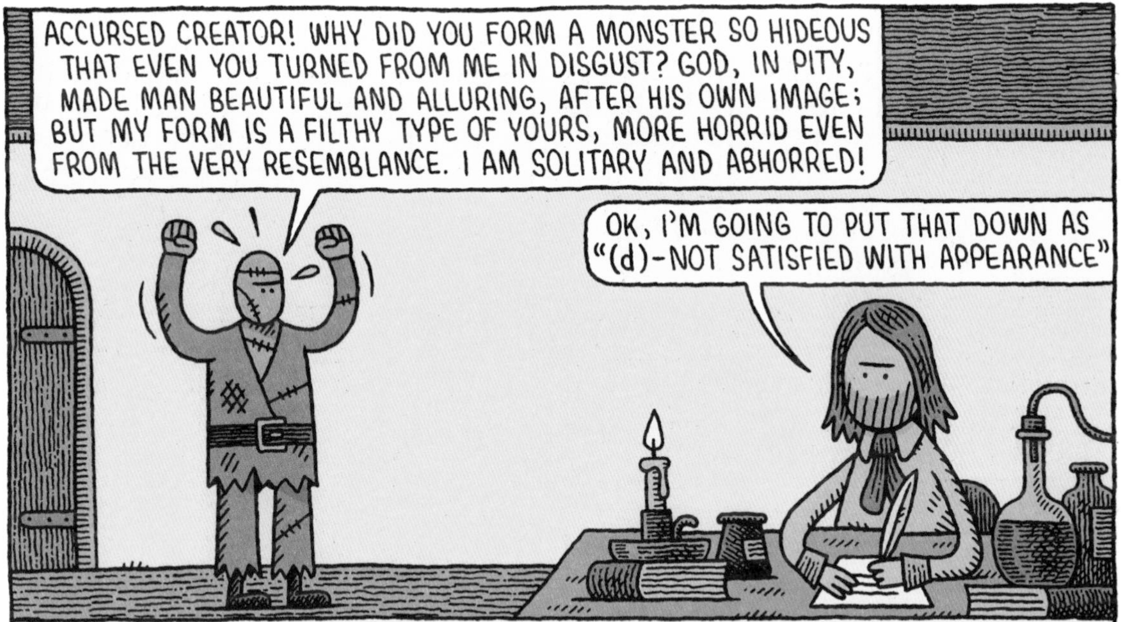
ACCURSED CREATOR! WHY DID YOU FORM A MONSTER SO HIDEOUS THAT EVEN YOU TURNED FROM ME IN DISGUST? GOD, IN PITY, MADE MAN BEAUTIFUL AND ALLURING, AFTER HIS OWN IMAGE; BUT MY FORM IS A FILTHY TYPE OF YOURS, MORE HORRID EVEN FROM THE VERY RESEMBLANCE. I AM SOLITARY AND ABHORRED!
OK, I'M GOING TO PUT THAT DOWN AS "(d)-NOT SATISFIED WITH APPEARANCE"
DOCTOR FRANKENSTEIN FILLS OUT A POST-EXPERIMENT ANALYSIS REPORT

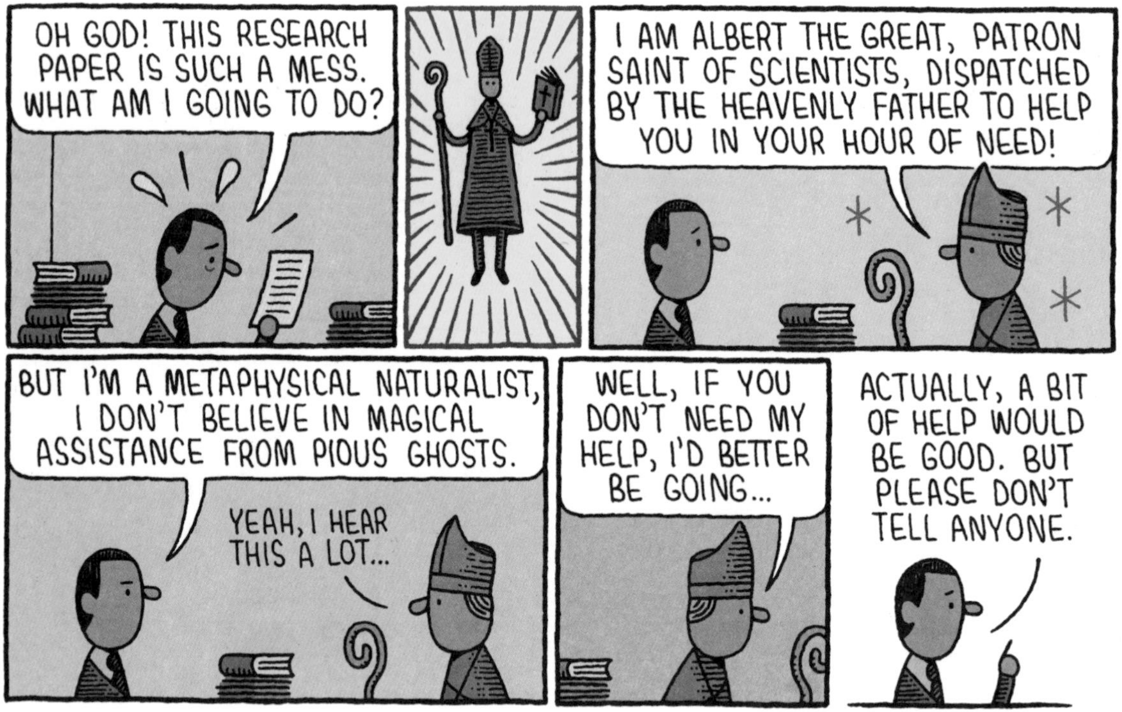
OH GOD! THIS RESEARCH PAPER IS SUCH A MESS. WHAT AM I GOING TO DO?
I AM ALBERT THE GREAT, PATRON SAINT OF SCIENTISTS, DISPATCHED BY THE HEAVENLY FATHER TO HELP YOU IN YOUR HOUR OF NEED!
BUT I'M A METAPHYSICAL NATURALIST, I DON'T BELIEVE IN MAGICAL ASSISTANCE FROM PIOUS GHOSTS.
YEAH, I HEAR THIS A LOT...
WELL, IF YOU DON'T NEED MY HELP, I'D BETTER BE GOING...
ACTUALLY, A BIT OF HELP WOULD BE GOOD. BUT PLEASE DON'T TELL ANYONE.

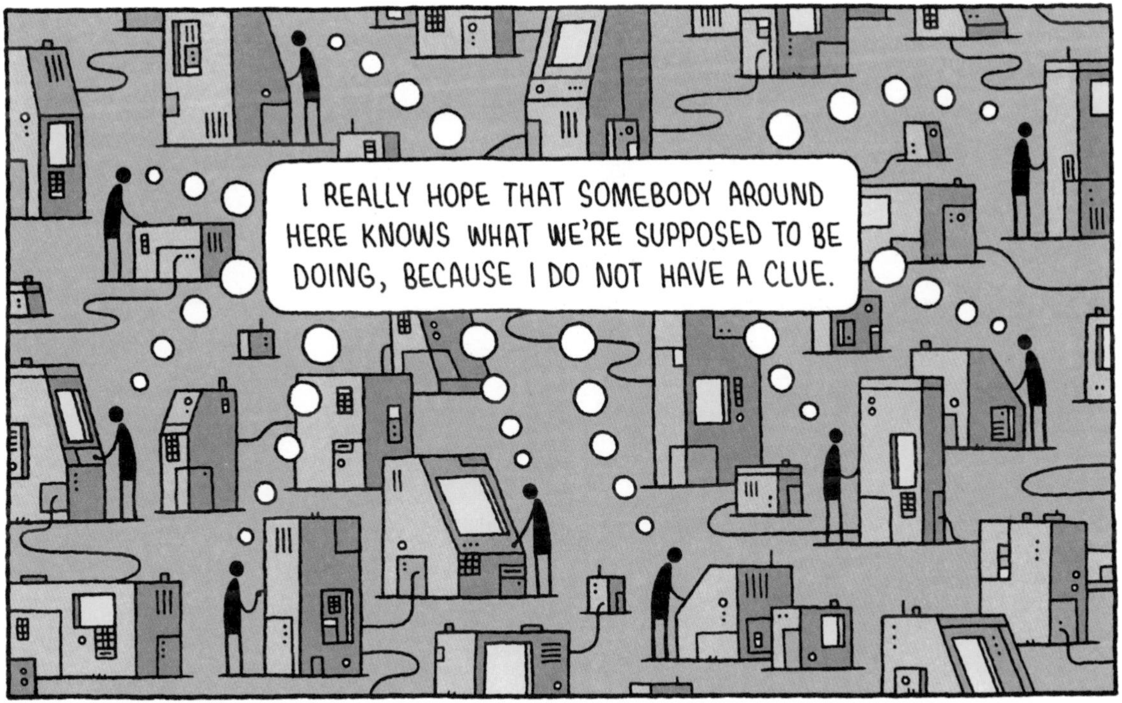
I REALLY HOPE THAT SOMEBODY AROUND HERE KNOWS WHAT WE'RE SUPPOSED TO BE DOING, BECAUSE I DO NOT HAVE A CLUE.

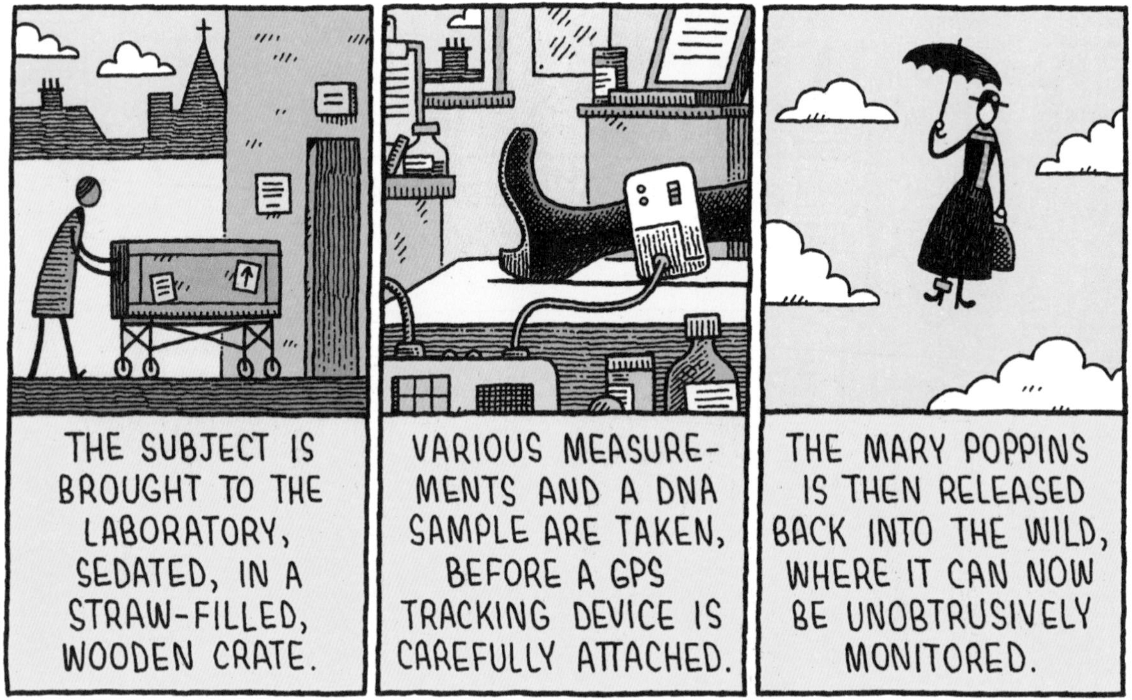
THE SUBJECT IS BROUGHT TO THE LABORATORY, SEDATED, IN A STRAW-FILLED, WOODEN CRATE.
VARIOUS MEASUREMENTS AND A DNA SAMPLE ARE TAKEN, BEFORE A GPS TRACKING DEVICE IS CAREFULLY ATTACHED.
THE MARY POPPINS IS THEN RELEASED BACK INTO THE WILD, WHERE IT CAN NOW BE UNOBTRUSIVELY MONITORED.

SIR ISAAC NEWTON, 1676

IF I HAVE SEEN FURTHER THAN OTHER MEN, IT IS BY STANDING ON THE SHOULDERS OF GIANTS...
LEANING IN CLOSE TO THEIR EARS AND SINGING THEM TO SLEEP
SO I CAN STEAL THEIR MAGIC GEESE AND USE THE PROCEEDS FROM THE SALE OF GOLDEN EGGS
TO FUND THE BUILDING OF A HUGE MECHANICAL INSECT WITH TELESCOPES FOR EYES.

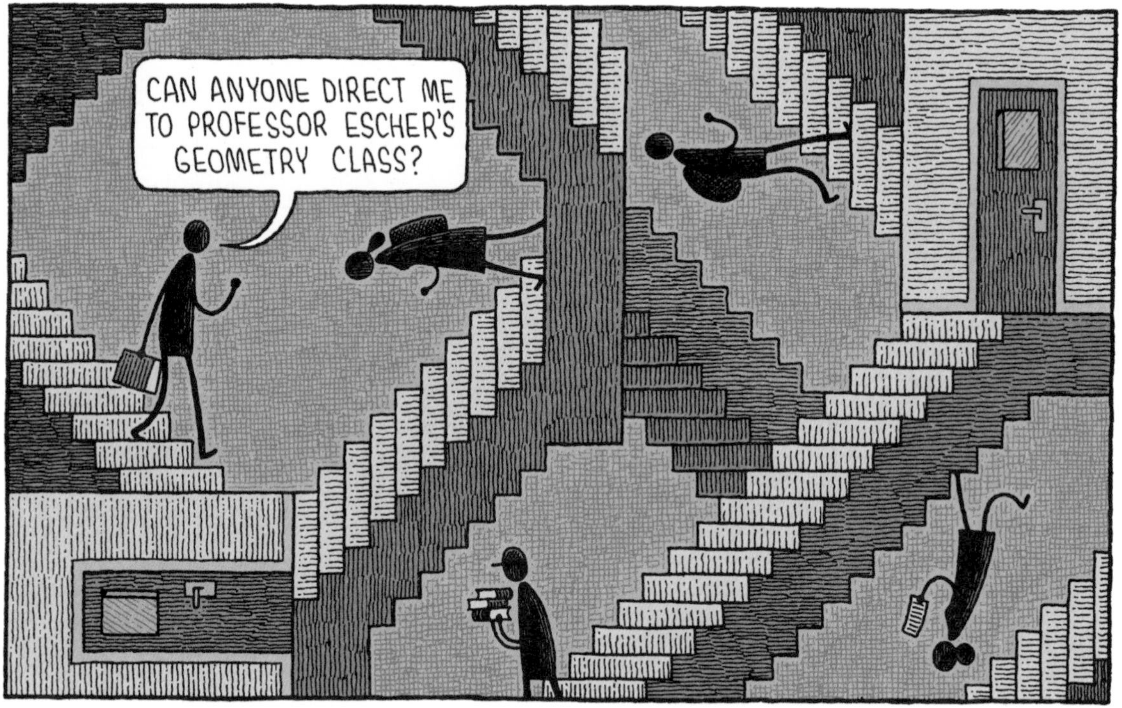
CAN ANYONE DIRECT ME TO PROFESSOR ESCHER'S GEOMETRY CLASS?

GREAT SCIENTIFIC MOMENTS IN OPERA

ACT III OF SCALPELLINO'S "THE UNFORTUNATE BIOLOGIST"	ACT II OF NEUSTADT'S "THE SHOCKING THEORY"	ACT IV OF CARAMICO'S "THE CHEMIST OF BOLOGNA"

MARIA FINALLY RECEIVES THE DELAYED LETTER AND SINGS THE HEARTBREAKING ARIA "PERCHÉ AVERMI RIFIUTATO UNA SOVVENZIONE?" ("WHY HAS MY GRANT PROPOSAL BEEN REJECTED?").	HELMUT, CAST OUT OF THE UNIVERSITY, EXPLAINS HIS IDEAS TO A CHORUS OF BEMUSED WOODCUTTERS, WHILE HIS TRUE LOVE HILDEGARD LISTENS FROM BEHIND AN OAK TREE.	LUCREZIA REALISES THAT THE MYSTERIOUS LAB ASSISTANT IS FEDERICO, AND THE PAIR SING THE CHARMING DUET "SCRIVIAMO SUBITO UN SAGGIO!" ("LET US CO-AUTHOR A PAPER AT ONCE!").

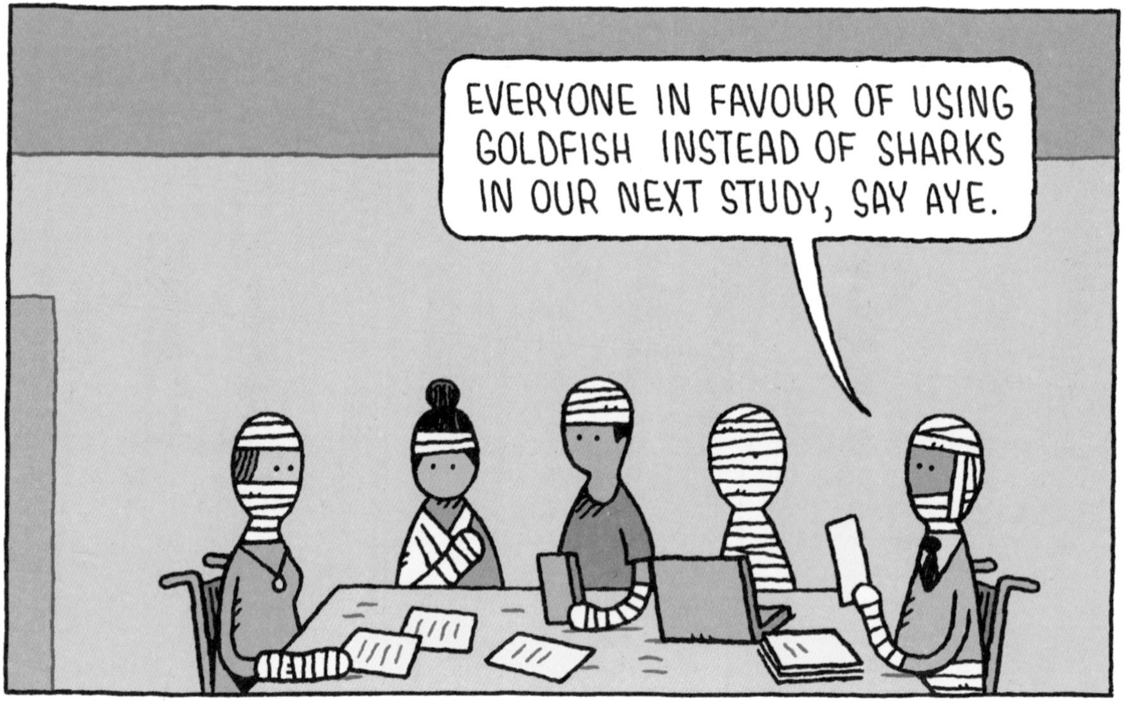
EVERYONE IN FAVOUR OF USING GOLDFISH INSTEAD OF SHARKS IN OUR NEXT STUDY, SAY AYE.

THESE CARTOONS ORIGINALLY APPEARED IN NEW SCIENTIST MAGAZINE.
I WOULD LIKE TO THANK CRAIG MACKIE, KATHRYN BRAZIER,
SUMIT PAUL-CHOUDHURY, PEGGY BURNS, TOM DEVLIN, TRACY HURREN,
JULIA POHL-MIRANDA, FRANCIS BICKMORE, JAMIE BYNG, CHARLOTTE BEVAN,
DAPHNE GAULD, IRIS GAULD, RON GAULD, SUSI GAULD, AND JO TAYLOR.

TOM GAULD WAS BORN IN 1976 AND GREW UP IN ABERDEENSHIRE,
SCOTLAND. HE IS A CARTOONIST AND ILLUSTRATOR AND HIS WORK IS
PUBLISHED IN THE GUARDIAN, THE NEW YORKER AND NEW SCIENTIST.
HIS COMIC BOOKS, 'BAKING WITH KAFKA', 'MOONCOP', 'YOU'RE ALL JUST
JEALOUS OF MY JETPACK', AND 'GOLIATH' ARE PUBLISHED BY
DRAWN & QUARTERLY. HE LIVES IN LONDON WITH HIS FAMILY.

WWW.TOMGAULD.COM

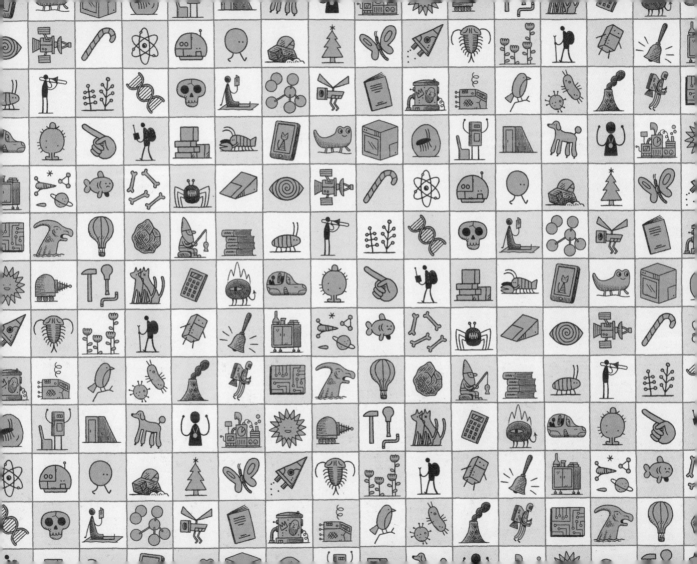

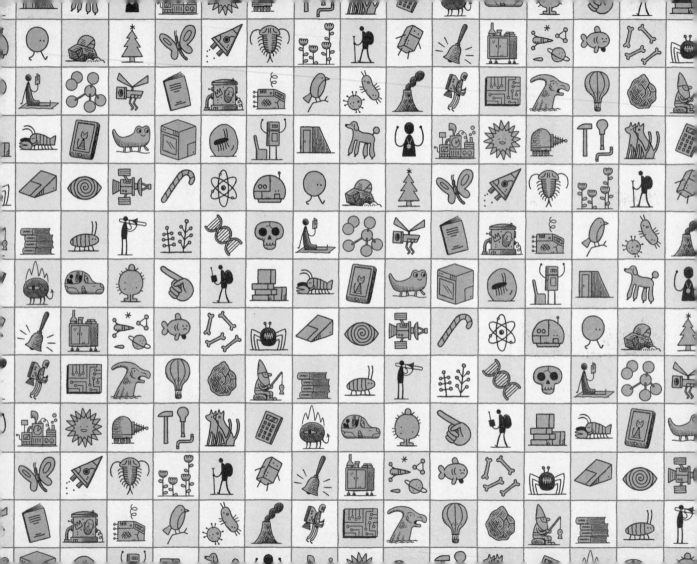